ENID

was born in 1889. Part o⟨...⟩
Jamaica ; later she was edu⟨...⟩
Germany, and in Paris. Sh⟨...⟩
an art student at Walter Sic⟨...⟩ng and
painting ; her friends includ⟨...⟩ such legendary figures as
Gaudier-Brzeska, Lovat Fraser, Katherine Mansfield,
Frank Harris. At the outbreak of war she went to work
as a VAD nurse at the Royal Herbert Hospital, Wool-
wich – *A Diary Without Dates*, her first book, recounts
her experiences there. Later she joined the First Aid
Nursing Yeomanry, serving in France as a driver : she
made that period the subject of *The Happy Foreigner*, her
second novel (1920). In the same year she married Sir
Roderick Jones, Chairman of Reuters ; they had four
children. Other novels are *Serena Blandish* (1924), a
children's book, *Alice and Thomas and Jane* (1930), the
world famous *National Velvet* (1935), *The Squire* (1938),
The Loved and Envied (1951) and *The Girl's Journey*
(1954).
Enid Bagnold is also a distinguished playwright. Her
nine plays include, notably, *The Chalk Garden* (1956)
and *The Chinese Prime Minister* (1964). Enid Bagnold
published her *Autobiography* in 1969 and lives in Sussex.

VIRAGO

is a feminist publishing company:

"It is only when women start to organise
in large numbers that we become a
political force, and begin to move towards
the possibility of a truly democratic society
in which every human being can be brave,
responsible, thinking and diligent in the struggle
to live at once freely and unselfishly"

SHEILA ROWBOTHAM
Women, Resistance and Revolution

VIRAGO
Advisory Group

A Diary Without Dates

Also by ENID BAGNOLD

PROSE:

The Happy Foreigner
Serena Blandish: or the Difficulty of Getting Married
Alice and Thomas and Jane
National Velvet
The Squire
The Loved and Envied
The Girl's Journey (reprint)

PLAYS:

Lottie Dundass
National Velvet
Poor Judas
Gertie
The Chalk Garden
The Last Joke
The Chinese Prime Minister
Call Me Jacky
Four Plays (*The Chalk Garden*, *The Last Joke*, *The Chinese Prime Minister* and *Call Me Jacky* in one volume)

POETRY:

Sailing Ships

TRANSLATION:

Alexander of Asia (*Alexandre Asiatique* by Princesse Marthe Bibesco)

A Diary
Without Dates

By Enid Bagnold

With a new introduction
by Monica Dickens

Published in association with
William Heinemann Limited

Virago

London

Facsimile Edition

Published by VIRAGO Limited 1978
5 Wardour Street, London W1V 3HE
in association with William Heinemann Limited

First published 1918 by William Heinemann Limited

ISBN 0 86068 036 3

Printed in Great Britain by litho at
The Anchor Press, Tiptree, Essex

I

INTRODUCTION

Anyone who read this short gem of a book when it was first published in 1918 must have felt that this new young writer had extraordinary talent and perception. We know that for sure now, from Enid Bagnold's other work, but still, if there were only this . . .

She was a V.A.D. in a hospital in England in the First World War, a very junior nurse, subservient to the rules and caprices of the almighty Sisters, aching with helpless pity for the pain brought back from the trenches to be endured, in those days before efficient analgesics and control of sepsis.

'To stand upright on one's feet, strong, easy without the surging of any physical sensation, by a bedside whose coverings are flung here and there by the quivering nerves beneath it . . . there is a sort of shame in such strength.

' "What can I do for you?" my eyes cry dumbly into his clouded brown pupils.

'By the fire, the Ward Sister was drinking tea

and laughing with the M.O.

' "The officer in No. 22 says he's in great pain . . ."'

' "I know," she said quite decently, "but I can't do anything. He must stick it out." '

There were so few drugs, and grudgingly given. The pain, so poignantly described by this very young V.A.D. who had never yet known it, was a permanent presence in the wards where dressings were a daily visit to hell, and a six-inch wound cavity had to be probed and plugged without gas, because 'the anaesthetist couldn't be found'.

He must stick it out. In my war, almost thirty years later, pain killers were still grudged, as if part of the cure was the purge of suffering, and you could never find a night nurse senior enough to possess the key to the celestial drug cupboard.

My Sisters were not so different from Enid Bagnold's flock of inured, dedicated women to whom the officers were almost men and the soldiers all facelessly 'the boys', content only when the bedspread corners were sharp as white cardboard. I know her soundless cry: 'Are we here to help the Sisters or the patients?', and I know that pouring her thoughts and emotions into her diary without dates was probably the thing that saved her. And her humour, and her quiet joy in watching.

She watches the dairyman, now a cavalryman, going crazy from fear of horses, the eyeless, noseless man who Sister says is 'Not up to much', jokey Pinker with the hideous girl friend from the Mile End Road, the lady visitor with her impertinent inquiries after the souls of the Tommies – they all called each other Bill – and the fledgling V.A.D., hungry, sick, aching, poor camel, waiting for the last straw.

'With me,' veteran Nurse Enid writes, 'the sickness and the hunger and the ache are barely remembered. It makes me wonder what else is left behind . . . The old battle is again in my mind – the struggle to feel pain, to repel the invading familiarity.' Not to get like the Sisters. One slaved to pass exams and put in time to become senior, but ahead was the fear : will I get like them? When Nurse Enid's drudgery was transformed by a brief, magical love affair with 'No. 11', they shipped him out quickly to another hospital.

No wonder that beneath the natural quiet delight of a writer born to watch and record, this is a sad little book.

The images are haunting. 'The hospital is like a dream. I am afraid of waking up and finding it commonplace. The white sisters, the ceaselessly changing patients, the long passages, the sudden plunges into the brilliant wards . . . their scenery hypnotises me . . . The long corridor, dim and lonely, the light centred in the gleam of the trays, salt-cellars, yellow butters, cylinders of glass.' She pauses, a bunch of forks in hand, to watch a stretcher go empty into a ward and come out bearing something under a flag. On summer evenings, there are regiments of charwomen, abreast upon their knees. In winter, fog swirls down the corridor from the spartanly open windows. By the dispensary hatch, the V.A.D.s gossip with their straw baskets like women at a market until the hatch is flung up by one of the three crotchety old bachelors who hoard the pills.

Images flicker in and out of the brief diary passages. Her touch is delicate and exact. The distilled essence of a scene, a snatch of dialogue that hangs in the air like the nurses' breath in the icy corridor, three bars of accordion music from the T.B. ward. The whole miniature world of the hospital, self-absorbed, unreal, as hospitals are, yet through the eyes of this watching, pitying, enamoured girl, more real to us at this distance than the reality.

1978   Monica Dickens

TO
THAT FRIEND OF MINE
WHO, WHEN I WROTE HIM
ENDLESS LETTERS,
SAID COLDLY,
"WHY NOT KEEP SOMETHING
FOR YOURSELF!"

I apologize to those whom I may hurt.

Can I soothe them by pleading that one may only write what is true for oneself?

E. B.

CONTENTS

I

OUTSIDE THE GLASS DOORS

I

OUTSIDE THE GLASS DOORS

I LIKE discipline. I like to be part of an institution. It gives one more liberty than is possible among three or four observant friends.

It is always cool and wonderful after the monotony of the dim hospital, its half-lit corridors stretching as far as one can see, to come out into the dazzling starlight and climb the hill, up into the trees and shrubberies here.

The wind was terrible to-night. I had to battle up, and the leaves were driven down the hill so fast that once I thought it was a motor-bicycle.

Madeleine's garden next door is all deserted now: they have gone up to London. The green asphalt tennis-court is shining with rain, the blue pond brown with slime; the little statues and bowls are lying on their sides to keep the wind from putting them forcibly there; and all over the house are white draperies and ghost chairs.

When I walk in the garden I feel like a ghost left over from the summer too.

I became aware to-night of one face detaching

itself from the rest. It is not a more pleasing face than the others, but it is becoming conspicuous to me.

Twice a week, when there is a concert in the big hall, the officers and the V.A.D.'s are divided, by some unspoken rule—the officers sitting at one side of the room, the V.A.D.'s in a white row on the other.

When my eyes rest for a moment on the motley of dressing-gowns, mackintoshes, uniforms, I inevitably see in the line one face set on a slant, one pair of eyes forsaking the stage and fixed on me in a steady, inoffensive beam.

This irritates me. The very lack of offence irritates me. But one grows to look for everything.

Afterwards in the dining-room during Mess he will ask politely: "What did you think of the concert, Sister? Good show. . . ."

How wonderful to be called Sister! Every time the uncommon name is used towards me I feel the glow of an implied relationship, something which links me to the speaker.

My Sister remarked: "If it's only a matter of that, we can provide thrills for you here very easily."

The name of my . . . admirer . . . is, after all, Pettitt. The other nurse in the Mess, who is very grand and insists on pronouncing his name in the French way, says he is "of humble origin."

He seems to have no relations and no visitors.

OUTSIDE THE GLASS DOORS

Out in the corridor I meditate on love.

Laying trays soothes the activity of the body, and the mind works softly.

I meditate on love. I say to myself that Mr. Pettitt is to be envied. I am still the wonder of the unknown to him: I exist, walk, talk, every day beneath the beam of his eye, impenetrable.

He fell down again yesterday, and his foot won't heal. He has time before him.

But in a hospital one has never time, one is never sure. He has perhaps been here long enough to learn that—to feel the insecurity, the impermanency.

At any moment he may be forced to disappear into the secondary stage of convalescent homes.

Yes, the impermanency of life in a hospital! An everlasting dislocation of combinations.

Like nuns, one must learn to do with no nearer friend than God.

Bolts, in the shape of sudden, whimsical orders, are flung by an Almighty whom one does not see.

The Sister who is over me, the only Sister who can laugh at things other than jokes, is going in the first week of next month. Why? Where? She doesn't know, but only smiles at my impatience. She knows life—hospital life.

It unsettles me as I lay my spoons and forks. Sixty-five trays. It takes an hour to do. Thirteen pieces on each tray. Thirteen times sixty-five . . .

eight hundred and forty-five things to collect, lay, square up symmetrically. I make little absurd reflections and arrangements—taking a dislike to the knives because they will not lie still on the polished metal of the tray, but pivot on their shafts, and swing out at angles after my fingers have left them.

I love the long, the dim and lonely, corridor; the light centred in the gleam of the trays, salt-cellars, yellow butters, cylinders of glass. . . .

Impermanency. . . . I don't wonder the Sisters grow so secret, so uneager. How often stifled! How often torn apart!

It's heaven to me to be one of such a number of faces.

To see them pass into Mess like ghosts—gentleman, tinker, and tailor; each having shuffled home from death; each having known his life rock on its base . . . not talking much—for what is there to say?—not laughing much, for they have been here too long—is a nightly pleasure to me.

Creatures of habit! All the coloured dressing-gowns range themselves round the two long tables—this man in this seat, that man by the gas-fire; this man with his wheel-chair drawn up at the end, that man at the corner where no one will jostle his arm.

Curious how these officers leave the hospital, so silently. Disappearances. . . . One face after another slips out of the picture, the unknown heart behind the face fixed intently on some other centre of life.

I went into a soldiers' ward to-night to inquire about a man who has pneumonia.

Round his bed there stood three red screens, and the busy, white-capped heads of two Sisters bobbed above the rampart.

It suddenly shocked me. What were they doing there? Why the screens? Why the look of strain in the eyes of the man in the next bed who could see behind the screens?

I went cold and stood rooted, waiting till one of them could come out and speak to me.

Soon they took away the screen nearest to me; they had done with it.

The man I was to inquire for has no nostrils; they were blown away, and he breathes through two pieces of red rubber tubing: it gave a more horrible look to his face than I have ever seen.

The Sister came out and told me she thought he was "not up to much." I think she means he is dying.

I wonder if he thinks it better to die. . . . But he was nearly well before he got pneumonia, had begun to take up the little habits of living. He had been out to tea.

Inexplicable, what he thinks of, lying behind the screen.

7

To-night I was laying my trays in the corridor, the dim corridor that I am likely often to mention —the occasional blue gas-lamps hanging at intervals down the roof in a dwindling perspective.

The only unshaded light in the corridor hangs above my head, making the cutlery gleam in my hands.

The swish-swish of a lame foot approached down the stone tiling with the tapping, soft and dull, of a rubber-tipped walking-stick.

He paused by the pillar, as I knew he would, and I busied myself with an added rush and hurry, an added irritating noise of spoons flung down.

He waited patiently, shyly. I didn't look up, but I knew his face was half smiling and suppliant.

"We shall miss you," he said.

"But I shall be back in a week!"

"We shall miss you . . . laying the trays out here."

"Everything passes," I said gaily.

He whistled a little and balanced himself against his stick.

"You are like me, Sister," he said earnestly; and I saw that he took me for a philosopher.

He shuffled on almost beyond the circle of light, paused while my lips moved in a vague smile of response, then moved on into the shadow. The low, deep quiet of the corridor resumed its hold on me. The patter of reflection in my brain proceeded undisturbed.

"You are like me!" The deepest flattery one creature pays its fellow . . . the cry which is uttered when another enters "our country."

Far down the corridor a slim figure in white approaches, dwarfed by the smoky distance; her nun-like cap floating, her scarlet cape, the "cape of pride," slipped round her narrow shoulders.

How intent and silent They are!

I watched this one pass with a look half reverence, half envy. One should never aspire to know a Sister intimately. They are disappointing people; without candour, without imagination. Yet what a look of personality hangs about them. . . .

To-night . . . Mr. Pettitt: "Sister!"

"Yes, Mr. Pettitt."

"Do you ever go to theatres? Do you like them?"

At the risk of appearing unnatural, I said, "Not much."

"Oh . . . I thought . . . H'm, that's a pity. Don't you like revues?"

"Oh, yes. . . ."

"I thought you'd take me to a *matinée* one afternoon."

"Oh, charming! I can't get leave in the afternoons, though."

"You often have a day off."

"Yes, but it's too soon to ask for another."

"Well, how about Wednesday, then?"

"Too soon. Think of the new Sister, and her opinion of me! That has yet to be won."

"Well, let me know, anyway. . . ."

(Staved off!)

The new Sister is coming quite soon: she has a medal.

Now that I know *my* Sister must go I don't talk to her much; I almost avoid her. That's true hospital philosophy.

I must put down the beauty of the night and the woman's laugh in the shadowy hedge. . . .

I walked up from the hospital late to-night, half-past eight, and hungry . . . in the cold, brilliant moonlight; a fine moon, very low, throwing long, pointed shadows across the road from the trees and hedges.

As one climbs up there is a wood on the right, the remains of the old wooded hill; sparse trees, very tall; and to-night a star between every branch, and a fierce moon beating down on the mud and grass.

I had on my white cap and long blue coat, very visible. The moon swept the road from side to side: lovers, acting as though it were night, were lit as though it was day.

OUTSIDE THE GLASS DOORS

I turned into the wood to take a message to a house set back from the road, and the moonlight and the night vapour rising from the marshy ground were all tangled together so that I could hardly see hedge from field or path.

I saw a lit cigarette-end, and a woman's laugh came across the field as naturally as if a sheep had bleated in the swampy grass. It struck me that the dark countryside was built to surround and hide a laugh like hers—the laugh of a lover, animal and protesting.

I saw the glowing end of the cigarette dance in a curve and fall to the ground, and she laughed again more faintly.

Walking on in the middle of the moonlight, I reached the gate I was looking for, ran up the pebbly drive to the dining-room window, gave my message, and returned.

I slipped my cap off my hair and pushed it into my pocket, keeping under the shadow of the hedge and into the quiet field.

They were whispering: "Do you?" "I do . . ." "Are you?" "I am . . ." crushed into the wet branches of the hedge.

The Mess went vilely to-night. Sister adds up on her fingers, and that's fatal, so all the numbers were out, and the *chef* sent in forty-five meats instead of fifty-one. I blushed with horror and responsibility, standing there watching six hungry men pretending to be philosophers.

The sergeant wolfed the cheese too. He got it out from under my very eyes while I was clearing the tables and ate it, standing up to it in the pantry with his back to me when I went in to fetch a tray.

Whenever I see that broad khaki back, the knickered legs astride, the flexed elbow-tips, I know that his digestion is laying up more trouble for him.

Benks, the Mess orderly, overeats himself too. He comes to the bunk and thrusts his little smile round the door: "Sister, I got another of them sick 'eadaches," very cheerfully, as though he had got something worth having. She actually retorted, "Benks, you eat too much!" one day, but he only swung on one leg and smiled more cheerfully than ever.

The new Sister has come. That should mean a lot. What about one's habits of life . . . ?

The new Sister has come, and at present she is absolutely without personality, beyond her medal. She appears to be deaf.

I went along to-night to see and ask after the man who has his nose blown off.

After the long walk down the corridor in almost total darkness, the vapour of the rain floating through every open door and window, the sudden brilliancy of the ward was like a haven.

The man lay on my right on entering—the screen removed from him.

Far up the ward the Sister was working by a bed. Ryan, the man with his nose gone, was lying high on five or six pillows, slung in his position by tapes and webbing passed under his arms and attached to the bedposts. He lay with his profile to me—only he has no profile, as we know a man's. Like an ape, he has only his bumpy forehead and his protruding lips—the nose, the left eye, gone.

He was breathing heavily. They don't know yet whether he will live.

When a man dies they fetch him with a stretcher, just as he came in; only he enters with a blanket over him, and a flag covers him as he goes out. When he came in he was one of a convoy, but every man who can stand rises to his feet as he goes out. Then they play him to his funeral, to a grass mound at the back of the hospital.

It takes all sorts to make a hospital.

For instance, the Visitors. . . .

There is the lady who comes in to tea and wants to be introduced to everyone as though it was a school-treat.

She jokes about the cake, its scarcity or its quantity, and makes a lot of "fun" about two lumps of sugar.

When she is at her best the table assumes a perfect and listening silence—not the silence of the critic, but the silence of the absorbed child treasuring every item of talk for future use. After she goes the joy of her will last them all the evening.

There is the lady who comes in to tea and, sitting down at the only unlaid table, cries, "Nurse! I have no knife or plate or cup; and I prefer a glass of boiling water to tea. And would you mind sewing this button on my glove?"

There is the lady who comes in and asks the table at large: "I wonder if any one knows General Biggens? I once met him . . ."

Or: "You've been in Gallipoli? Did you run across my young cousin, a lieutenant in the . . . ? Well, he was only there two days or so, I suppose . . ." exactly as though she was talking about Cairo in the season.

To-day there was the Limit.

She sat two paces away from where I sit to pour out tea. Her face was kind, but inquisitive, with that brown liver-look round the eyes and a large rakish hat. She comes often, having heard of him through the *padre*, to see a Canadian whom she doesn't know and who doesn't want to see her.

From two places away I heard her voice piping up: "Nurse, excuse my asking, but is your cap a regulation one, like all the others?"

I looked up, and all the tea I was pouring poured over the edge. Mr. Pettitt and Captain Matthew, between us, looked down at their plates.

I put my hand to my cap. "Is anything wrong? It ought to be like the others."

She leant towards me, nodding and smiling with *bonhomie*, and said flatteringly, "It's so prettily put on, I thought it was different."

And then (horror): "Don't you think nurse puts her cap on well?" she asked Captain Matthew, who, looking harder than ever at his plate and reddening to the ears, mumbled something which did not particularly commit him since it couldn't be heard.

The usual delighted silence began to creep round the table, and I tried wildly to divert her attention before our end became a stage and the rest of the table an audience.

"I think it's so nice to see you sitting down with them all," she cooed; "it's so cosy for them."

"Is your cup empty?" I said furiously, and held out my hand for it. But it wasn't, of course; she couldn't even do that for me.

She shook hands with me when she went away and said she hoped to come again. And she will.

There was once a lady who asked me very loudly whether I "saw many horrible sights," and "did the V.A.D.'s have to go to the funerals?"

And another who cried out with emotion when she saw the first officer limp in to Mess, "And can some of them *walk*, then?" Perhaps she thought they came in to tea on stretchers, with field-bandages on. She quivered all over, too, as she looked from one to the other, and I feel sure she went home and broke down, crying, "What an experience . . . the actual wounds!"

Shuffle, shuffle, up the corridor to-night, as I was laying my trays. Captain Matthew appeared in the circle of light, his arm and hand bound up and his pipe in his mouth.

He paused by me. "Well . . ." he said companionably, and lolled against a pillar.

"You've done well at tea in the way of visitors," I remarked. "Six, wasn't it?"

"Yes," he said, "and now I've got rid of 'em all, except one."

"Where's the one?"

"In there." He pointed with his pipe to the empty Mess-Room. "He's the father of a subaltern of mine who was killed."

"He's come to talk to you about it?"

"Yes."

But he seemed in no hurry to go in, waiting against the pillar and staring at the moving cutlery.

He waited almost three minutes, then he sighed and went in.

Biscuits to put out, cheese to put out. How wet this new cheese is, and fresh and good the little bits that fall off the edge! I never eat cheese at home, but here the breakings are like manna.

And pears, with the old shopman's trick, little,

bitten ones at the bottom, fine ones at the top. Soft sugar, lump sugar, coffee. As one stirs the coffee round in the tin the whole room smells of it, that brown, burnt smell.

And then to click the light on, let down the blind, stir the fire, close the door of the little bunk, and, looking round it, think what exhilaration of liberty I have here.

Let them pile on the rules, invent and insist; yet behind them, beneath them, I have that strong, secret liberty of an institution that runs like a wind in me and lifts my mind like a leaf.

So long as I conform absolutely, not a soul will glance at my thoughts—few at my face. I have only to be silent and conform, and I might be in so far a land that even the eye of God had lost me.

I took the plate of biscuits, the two plates of cheese, one in each hand and one balanced with a new skill on my arm, and carried them into the dining-room, where the tables were already laid and only one light kept on as yet for economy's sake.

Low voices. . . . There in the dimmest corner sat Captain Matthew, his chin dug deep in his grey dressing-gown, and beside him a little elderly man, his hat on his knees, his anxious, ordinary face turned towards the light.

A citizen . . . a baker or a brewer, tinker, tailor, or candlestick-maker . . . ?

There had been the buying of the uniform, the

visits to the camp in England, the parcels to send out—always the parcels—week by week. And now nothing; no more parcels, no more letters, silence.

Only the last hungry pickings from Captain Matthew's tired memory and nervous speech.

I turned away with a great shrinking.

In a very few minutes the citizen went past my bunk door, his hat in his hand, his black coat buttoned; taking back to his home and his family the last facts that he might ever learn.

At the end of the passage he almost collided with that stretcher which bears a flag.

Of the two, the stretcher moved me least.

My Sister is afraid of death. She told me so. And not the less afraid, she said, after all she has seen of it. That is terrible.

But the new Sister is afraid of life. She is shorter-sighted.

The rain has been pouring all day.

To-night it has stopped, and all the hill is steam and drizzle and black with the blackness that war has thrust upon the countryside.

My Sister has gone.

Two nights ago I went up to a dinner at Madeleine's and to stay the night. My Sister said, "Go and enjoy yourself!" And I did. It is very amusing, the change into rooms full of talk and light; I feel a glow of pleasure as I climb to the room Madeleine calls mine and find the reflection of the fire on the blue wall-paper.

The evening wasn't remarkable, but I came back full of descriptions to the bunk and Sister next day.

I was running on, inventing this and that, making her laugh, when suddenly I looked up, and she had tears in her eyes.

I wavered and came to a stop. She got up suddenly and moved about the room, and then with a muttered "Wash my hands," disappeared into the corridor.

I sat and thought: "Is it that she has her life settled, quietly continuous, and one breaks in . . . ? Does the wind from outside hurt?"

I regretted it all the evening.

Yesterday I arrived at the hospital and couldn't find the store-cupboard keys, then ran across to her room and tapped at the door. Her voice called "Come in!" and I found her huddled in an arm-chair, unnerved and white. I asked her for the keys, and when she gave them to me she held out her hand and said: "I'm going away to-morrow. They are sending me home; they say I'm ill."

I muttered something with a feeling of shock, and going back to my bunk I brooded.

The new Sister came in, and a new V.A.D. too, explaining that my former companion was now going into a ward.

A sense of desolation was in the air, a ruthlessness on the part of someone unknown. "Shuffle, shuffle . . . they shuffle us like cards!"

I rose and began to teach the new V.A.D. the subtle art of laying trays. She seemed stupid.

I didn't want to share my trays with her. I love them; they are my recreation. I hung over them idly, hardly laying down the spoons I held in my hand, but, standing with them, chivvied the new V.A.D. until her movements became flustered and her eye distraught.

She was very ugly. I thought: "In a day or two I shall get to like her, and then I shan't be able to chivvy her."

Out in the corridor came a tremendous tramping, boots and jingling metal. Two armed men with fixed bayonets arrived, headed by a sergeant. The sergeant paused and looked uncertainly this way and that, and then at me.

I guessed their destination. "In there," I nodded, pointing through a closed glass door, and the sergeant marched his men in and beyond the door.

An officer had been brought back under arrest; I had seen him pass with his escort. The rumour at tea had been that he had extended his two days' leave into three weeks.

The V.A.D. looked at me questioningly, but she didn't dare, and I couldn't bear, to start any elucidations on the subject.

I couldn't think; she worried me. Her odds and

ends of conversation pecked at me like a small bird. She told me a riddle which filled me with nausea, and finally a limerick which I had heard three times in the Mess.

I left her and went into the bunk.

Here the new Sister had installed herself, gentle and pink and full of quiet murmurs.

The rain, half snow, half sleet, dabbled against the window-pane, and I lifted the blind to watch the flakes stick and melt on the glass.

The V.A.D., her trays finished, appeared in the doorway. The little room seemed full of people.

"There's a concert," I said, looking at the V.A.D. with distaste.

She looked at me uncertainly: "Aren't you coming?"

"No," I said, "I've a note to write," forgetting that the new Sister might not allow such infringements. She gave no sign.

The V.A.D. gave in and disappeared concert-wards.

The Sister rose too and went out into the kitchen to consult with the *chef*.

I slipped out behind her and down the steps into the garden—into the wet, dark garden, down the channels that were garden-paths, and felt my way over to the Sisters' quarters.

My Sister hadn't moved. There by the gas-fire, her thin hand to her face, she sat as she had two hours before.

"Come in," she offered, "and talk to me."

Her collar, which was open, she tried to do up. It made a painful impression on me of weakness and the effort to be normal.

I remembered that she had once told me she was so afraid of death, and I guessed that she was suffering now from that terror.

But when the specialist is afraid, what can ignorance say . . . ?

Life in the bunk is wretched (except that the new V.A.D. tells fortunes by hands).

The new Sister is at the same time timid and dogged. She looks at me with a sidelong look and gives me little flips with her hand, as though (a) she thought I might break something and (b) that she might stave it off by playfulness.

Pain . . .

To stand up straight on one's feet, strong, easy, without the surging of any physical sensation, by a bedside whose coverings are flung here and there by the quivering nerves beneath it . . . there is a sort of shame in such strength.

"What can I do for you?" my eyes cry dumbly into his clouded brown pupils.

I was told to carry trays from a ward where I had never been before—just to carry trays, orderly's work, no more.

No. 22 was lying flat on his back, his knees

drawn up under him, the sheets up to his chin; his flat, chalk-white face tilted at the ceiling. As I bent over to get his untouched tray his tortured brown eyes fell on me.

"I'm in pain, Sister," he said.

No one has ever said that to me before in that tone.

He gave me the look that a dog gives, and his words had the character of an unformed cry.

He was quite alone at the end of the ward. The Sister was in her bunk. My white cap attracted his desperate senses.

As he spoke his knees shot out from under him with his restless pain. His right arm was stretched from the bed in a narrow iron frame, reminding me of a hand laid along a harp to play the chords, the fingers with their swollen green flesh extended across the strings; but of this harp his fingers were the slave, not the master.

"Shall I call your Sister?" I whispered to him.

He shook his head. "She can't do anything. I must just stick it out. They're going to operate on the elbow, but they must wait three days first."

His head turned from side to side, but his eyes never left my face. I stood by him, helpless, overwhelmed by his horrible loneliness.

Then I carried his tray down the long ward and past the Sister's bunk. Within, by the fire, she was laughing with the M.O. and drinking a cup of tea—a harmless amusement.

"The officer in No. 22 says he's in great pain,"
I said doubtfully. (It wasn't my ward, and Sisters
are funny.)

"I know," she said quite decently, "but I can't
do anything. He must stick it out."

I looked through the ward door once or twice
during the evening, and still his knees, at the far
end of the room, were moving up and down.

It must happen to the men in France that, living
so near the edge of death, they are more aware of
life than we are.

When they come back, when the post-war days
set in, will they keep that vision, letting it play
on life . . . or must it fade?

And some become so careless of life, so careless
of all the whims and personalities and desires that
go to make up existence, that one wrote to me:

"The only real waste is the waste of metal. The
earth will be covered again and again with Us.
The corn will grow again; the bread and meat can
be repeated. But this metal that has lain in the
earth for centuries, the formation of the beginning,
that men have sweated and grubbed for . . . that
is the waste."

What carelessness of worldly success they should
bring back with them!

Orderlies come and go up and down the
corridor. Often they carry stretchers—now and

then a stretcher with the empty folds of a flag flung across it.

Then I pause from laying my trays, and with a bunch of forks in my hand I stand still.

They take the stretcher into a ward, and while I wait I know what they are doing behind the screens which stand around a bed against the wall. I hear the shuffle of feet as the men stand to attention, and the orderlies come out again, and the folds of the flag have ballooned up to receive and embrace a man's body.

Where is he going?

To the mortuary.

Yes . . . but where else . . . ?

Perhaps there is nothing better than the ecstasy and unappeasement of life?

II

INSIDE THE GLASS DOORS

INSIDE THE GLASS DOORS

My feet ache, ache, ache . . . !
End of the first day.

Life in a ward is all scurry and rush. I don't
reflect; I'm putting on my cap anyhow, and my
hands are going to the dogs.

I shall never get to understand Sisters; they
are so strange, so tricky, uncertain as collies. Deep
down they have an ineradicable axiom: that any
visitor, anyone in an old musquash coat, in a high-
boned collar, in a spotted veil tied up at the sides,
anyone with whom one shakes hands or takes tea,
is more important than the most charming patient
(except, of course, a warded M.O.).

For this reason the "mouths" of the pillow-
cases are all turned to face up the ward, away
from the door.

I think plants in a ward are a barbarism, for
as they are always arranged on the table by the
door, it is again obvious that they are intended
only to minister to the eye of the visitor, that race
of gods.

In our ward there are eighteen fern-pots, some

in copper, some in pink china, three in mauve paper, and one hanging basket of ferns. All of these have to be taken out on the landing at night and in again in the morning, and they have to be soaked under the tap.

The Sisters' minds are as yet too difficult for me, but in the minds of the V.A.D.'s I see certain salient features. I see already manifested in them the ardent longing to be alike. I know and remember this longing; it was present through all my early years in a large boarding-school; but there it was naturally corrected by the changes of growth and the inexpertness of youth. Here I see for the first time grown women trying with all the concentration of their fuller years to be as like one another as it is possible to be.

There is a certain dreadful innocence about them too, as though each would protest, "In spite of our tasks, our often immodest tasks, our minds are white as snow."

And, as far as I can see, their conception of a white female mind is the silliest, most mulish, incurious, unresponsive, condemning kind of an ideal that a human creature could set before it.

At present I am so humble that I am content to do all the labour and take none of the temperatures, but I can see very well that it is when I reach a higher plane that all the trouble will begin.

The ranklings, the heart-burnings, the gross injustices. . . . Who is to make the only poultice?

Who is to paint the very septic throat of Mr. Mullins, Army Service Corps? Who is to—dizzy splendour—go round with the M.O. should the Sister be off for a half-day?

These and other questions will form the pride and anguish of my inner life.

It is wonderful to go up to London and dine and stay the night with Madeleine after the hospital.

The hospital—a sort of monotone, a place of whispers and wheels moving on rubber tyres, long corridors, and strangely unsexed women moving in them. Unsexed not in any real sense, but the white clothes, the hidden hair, the stern white collar just below the chin, give them an air of school-girlishness, an air and a look women don't wear in the world. They seem unexpectant.

Then at Madeleine's . . . the light, the talk, the deep bath got ready for me by a maid, instead of my getting it ready for a patient. . . .

Not that I mind getting it ready; I like it. Only the change! It's like being turn and turn about maid and mistress.

There is the first snow here, scanty and frozen on the doorstep.

I came home last night in the dark to dinner and found its faint traces on the road and in the gutter as I climbed the hill. I couldn't see well; there were stars, but no moon. Higher up it was unmistakable; long white tracks frozen in the dried mud of the road, and a branch under a lamp thickened with frozen snow.

Shall I ever grow out of that excitement over the first bit of snow . . . ?

I felt a glow of pride in the hill, thinking:

"In London it's all slush and mud. They don't suspect what we've got here. A suburb is a wonderful place!"

After a wet and muddy day in London I've seen the trains pull into Charing Cross with snow piled on the roofs of the carriages, and felt a foot taller for joy that I was one of those fortunates who might step into a train and go down into a white countryside.

It is the same excitement to wake up early to an overnight fall and see down the Dover Road for miles no foot of man printed, but only the birds' feet. Considering the Dover Road has been a highway since the Romans, it really is a fine moment when you realize its surface has suddenly become untrodden and unexplored as any jungle.

Alas, the amount of snow that has set me writing! . . . two bucketfuls in the whole garden!

When a Medical Officer goes sick, or, in other words, when an M.O. is warded, a very special and almost cynical expression settles on his face. Also the bedside manner of the Visiting

Officer is discarded as he reaches the bed of the sick M.O.

"My knees are very painful," says the sick M.O., but it is a despondent statement, not a plea for aid.

The Visiting Officer nods, but he does not suggest that they will soon be better.

They look at each other as weak human beings look, and:

"We might try . . . ?" says the Visiting Officer questioningly.

The M.O. agrees without conviction, and settles back on his pillows. Not for him the comfortable trust in the divine knowledge of specialists. He can endure like a dog, but without its faith in its master.

The particular M.O. whose knees are painful is, as a matter of fact, better now. He got up yesterday.

Mooning about the ward in a dressing-gown, he stared first out of one window into the fog and then out of another.

Finally, just before he got back into bed, he made an epigram.

"Nurse," he said, "the difference between being in bed and getting up is that in bed you do nothing, but when you get up there's nothing to do. . . ."

I tucked him up and put the cradle over his knees, and he added, "One gets accustomed to everything," and settled back happily with his reading-lamp, his French novel and his dictionary.

The fog developed all day yesterday, piling up white and motionless against the window-panes. As night fell a little air of excitement ran here and there amongst the V.A.D.'s.

"How shall we get home . . . ?" "Are the buses running?" "Oh no, the last one is stuck against the railings outside!" "My torch has run out. . . ."

By seven o'clock even the long corridor was as dim as the alley outside. No one thought of shutting the windows—I doubt whether they will shut . . . and the fog rolled over the sill in banks and round the open glass doors, till even the white cap of a Sister could hardly be seen as she passed.

I am pleased with any atmospheric exaggeration; the adventure of going home was before me. . . .

At eight I felt my way down over the steps into the alley; the torch, held low on the ground, lighted but a small, pale circle round my shoes. Outside it was black and solid and strangely quiet.

In the yard a man here and there raised his voice in a shout; feet strayed near mine and edged away.

At the cross-roads I came on a lantern standing upon the ground, and by it drooped the nose of a benighted horse; the spurt of a match lit the face of its owner.

Up the hill, the torch held low against the kerb-stone, the sudden looming of a black giant made me start back as I nearly ran my head into a telegraph-post. . . .

I was at the bottom of the sea; fathoms and fathoms of fog must stand above my head.

Suddenly a dozen lights showed about me, then the whole sky alight with stars, and naked trees with the rime on them, bristling; the long road ran up the hill its accustomed steel colour, the post office was there with its red window, the lean old lamp-post with its broken arm. . . .

I had walked out of the fog as one walks out of the sea on to a beach!

Looking back, I could see the pit behind me; the fog standing on the road like a solid wall, straight up and down. Again I felt a pride in the hill. "Down there," I thought, "those groping feet and shouting voices; that man and that horse . . . they don't guess!"

I walked briskly up the hill, and presently stepped on to the pavement; but at the edge of the asphalt, where tufted grass should grow, something crackled and hissed under my feet. Under the torchlight the unnatural grass was white and brittle with rime, fanciful as a stage fairy scene, and the railings beyond it glittered too.

I slid in the road as I turned down the drive; a sheet of ice was spread where the leaky pipe is, and the steps up to the house door were slippery.

But oh, the honeysuckle and the rose-trees . . . !
Bush, plant, leaf, stem, rimed from end to end.
The garden was a Bond Street jeweller's!

Perhaps the final chapter on Mr. Pettitt. . . .
In the excitement of the ward I had almost
forgotten him; he is buried in the Mess, in the
days when I lived on the floor below.

To-night, as I was waiting by the open hatch
of the kitchen for my tray to be filled with little
castles of lemon jelly, the hot blast from the
kitchen drawing stray wisps of hair from beneath
my cap, I saw the familiar limping figure—a figure
bound up with my first days at the hospital,
evoking a hundred evenings at the concerts, in
the dining-room. I felt he had been away, but I
didn't dare risk a "So you're back!"

He smiled, blushed, and limped past me.

Upstairs in the ward, as I was serving out my
jellies, he arrived in the doorway, but, avoiding
me, hobbled round the ward, visiting every bed
but the one I was at at the moment. Then he
went downstairs again.

I passed him on the stairs. He can't say he
didn't have his opportunity, for I even stopped
with my heavy tray and spoke to him.

Half an hour later he was back in the ward again
(not his ward), and this time he found the courage
of hysteria. There in the middle of the ward,
under the glaring Christmas lights, with the eyes

of every interested man in every bed glued upon us, he presented me with a fan wrapped in white paper: "A little present I bought you, nurse." I took it, eyes sizzling and burning holes in my shoulders, and stammered my frantic thanks.

"You do like it, nurse?" he said rapidly, three times in succession.

And I: "I do, I do, I do. . . ."

"I thought you would. You do like it?"

"Oh, just what I wanted!"

"That's all right, then. Just a little Christmas present."

We couldn't stop. It was like taking too much butter for the marmalade and too much marmalade for the butter.

He leaves the hospital in a day or two. .

The fog is still thick. To-night at the station after a day off I found it white and silent. Touching the arm of a man, I asked him the all-important question: "Are the buses running?"

"Oh, no . . ."

And the cabs all gone home to bed, and I was hungry!

What ghosts pass . . . and voices, bodyless, talking intimately while their feet fall without a stir on the grass of the open Heath.

I was excited by the strange silent fog.

But my left shoe began to hurt me, and stopping at the house of a girl I knew, I borrowed a country pair of hers: no taller than

I, she takes two sizes larger; they were like boats.

I started to trudge the three miles home in the boats: the slightest flick of the foot would have sent one of them flying beyond the eye of God or man. After a couple of miles the shoes began to tell, and I stood still and lifted up one foot behind me, craning over my shoulder to see if I could catch sight of the glimmer of skin through the heel of the stocking. The fog was too thick for that.

Another half-mile and I put my finger down to my heel and felt the wet blood through a large hole in my stocking, so I took off the shoes and tied them together . . . and, more silent than ever in the tomb of fog, passed along as God had first supposed that woman would walk, on the wet surface of the road.

A warded M.O. is pathetic. He knows he can't get well quicker than time will let him. He has no faith.

To-morrow I have to take down all the decorations that I put up for Christmas. When I put them up I never thought I should be the one to take them down. When I was born no one thought I should be old.

While I was untying a piece of holly from the electric-light cords on the ceiling and a patient was holding the ladder for me, a young *padre* came and pretended to help us, but while he stood with us he whispered to the patient, "Are you a communicant?" I felt a wave of heat and anger; I could have dropped the holly on him.

They hung up their stockings on Christmas night on walking-sticks hitched over the ends of the beds and under the mattresses. Such big stockings! Many of them must have played Father Christmas in their own homes, to their own children, on other Christmases.

On Christmas Eve I didn't leave the hospital till long after the Day-Sisters had gone and the Night-Sisters came on. The wards were all quiet as I walked down the corridor, and to left and right through the glass doors hung the rows of expectant stockings.

Final and despairing postscript on Mr. Pettitt. When a woman says she cannot come to lunch it is because she doesn't want to.

Let this serve as an axiom to every lover: A woman who refuses lunch refuses everything.

The hospital is alive; I feel it like a living being.

The hospital is like a dream. I am afraid of waking up and finding it commonplace.

The white Sisters, the ceaselessly-changing patients, the long passages, the sudden plunges into the brilliant wards . . . their scenery hypnotizes me.

Sometimes in the late evening one walks busily up and down the ward doing this and that, forgetting that there is anything beyond the drawn blinds, engrossed in the patients, one's tasks— bed-making, washing, one errand and another— and then suddenly a blind will blow out and almost up to the ceiling, and through it you will catch a glimpse that makes you gasp, of a black night crossed with bladed searchlights, of a moon behind a crooked tree.

The lifting of the blind is a miracle; I do not believe in the wind.

A new Sister on to-night . . . very severe. We had to make the beds like white cardboard. I wonder what she thinks of me.

Mr. Pettitt (who really is going to-morrow) wandered up into the ward and limped near me. "Sister . . ." he began. He *will* call me "Sister." I frowned at him. The new Sister glanced at him and blinked.

He was very persistent. "Sister," he said again, "do you think I can have a word with you?"

"Not now," I whispered as I hurried past him.

"Oh, is that so?" he said, as though I had made an interesting statement, and limped away, looking backwards at me. I suppose he wants to say good-bye.

INSIDE THE GLASS DOORS

He sat beside Mr. Wicks's bed (Mr. Wicks who is paralysed) and looked at me from time to time with that stare of his which contains so little offence.

It is curious to think that I once saw Mr. Wicks on a tennis-lawn, walking across the grass . . . Mr. Wicks, who will never put his foot on grass again, but, lying in his bed, continues to say, as all Tommies say, "I feel well in meself."

So he does; he feels well in himself. But he isn't going to live, all the same.

Still his routine goes on: he plays his game of cards, he has his joke: "Lemonade, please, nurse; but it's not from choice!"

When I go to clear his ash-tray at night I always say, "Well, now I've got something worth clearing at last!"

And he chuckles and answers: "Thought you'd be pleased. It's the others gets round my bed and leaves their bits."

He was once a sergeant: he got his commission a year ago.

My ruined charms cry aloud for help.

The cap wears away my front hair; my feet are widening from the everlasting boards; my hands won't take my rings.

I was advised last night on the telephone to marry immediately before it was too late.

A desperate remedy. I will try cold cream and hair tonics first.

There is a tuberculosis ward across the landing. They call it the T.B. ward.

It is a den of coughs and harrowing noises.

One night I saw a negro standing in the doorway with his long hair done up in hairpins. He is the pet of the T.B. ward; they call him Henry.

Henry came in to help us with our Christmas decorations on Christmas Eve, and as he cleverly made wreaths my Sister whispered to me, "He's never spitting . . . in the ward!"

But he wasn't, it was part of his language— little clicks and ticks. He comes from somewhere in Central Africa, and one of the T.B.'s told me, "He's only got one wife, nurse."

He is very proud of his austerity, for he has somehow discovered that he has hit on a country where it is the nutty thing only to have one wife.

No one can speak a word of his language, no one knows exactly where he comes from; but he can say in English, "Good morning, Sister!" and "Christmas Box!" and "One!"

Directly one takes any notice of him he laughs and clicks, holding up one finger, crying, "One!"

Then a proud T.B. (they regard him as the Creator might regard a humming-bird) explains: "He means he's only got one wife, nurse."

Then he did his second trick. He came to me with outstretched black hand and took my apron, fingering it. Its whiteness slipped between his fingers. He dropped it and, holding up the hand with its fellow, ducked his head to watch me with his glinting eyes.

"He means," explained the versatile T.B., "that he has ten piccaninnies in his village and they're all dressed in white."

It took my breath away; I looked at Henry for corroboration. He nodded earnestly, coughed and whispered, "Ten!"

"How do you know he means that?" I asked. "How can you possibly have found out?"

"We got pictures, nurse. We showed 'im kids, and 'e said 'e got ten—six girls and four boys. We showed 'im pictures of kids."

I had never seen Henry before, never knew he existed. But in the ward opposite the poor T.B.'s had been holding conversations with him in window-seats, showing him pictures, painfully establishing a communion with him . . . Henry, with his hair done up in hairpins!

Although they showed him off with conscious pride, I don't think he really appeared strange to them, beyond his colour. I believe they imagine his wife as appearing much as their own wives, his children as the little children who run about their own doorsteps. They do not stretch their imaginations to conceive any strangeness about his home surroundings to correspond with his own strangeness.

To them Henry has the dignity of a man and a householder, possibly a ratepayer.

He seems quite happy and amused. I see him carrying a bucket sometimes, sharing its handle with a flushed T.B. They carry on animated conversations as they go downstairs, the T.B. talking the most. It reminds me of a child and a dog.

What strange machinery is there for getting him back? Part of the cargo of a ship . . . one day . . . "a nigger for Central Africa. . . ."

"Where's his unit?"

"Who knows! One nigger and his bundle . . . for Central Africa!"

The ward has put Mr. Wicks to Coventry because he has been abusive and violent-tempered for three days.

He lies flat in his bed and frowns; no more jokes over the lemonade, no wilfulness over the thermometer.

It is in these days that Mr. Wicks faces the truth.

I lingered by his bed last night, after I had put his tea-tray on his table, and looked down at him; he pretended to be inanimate, his open eyes fixed upon the white rail of the bed. His bedclothes were stretched about him as though he had not moved since his bed was made, hours before.

His worldly pleasures were beside him—his

reading-lamp, his Christmas box of cigars, his *Star* —but his eyes, disregarding them, were upon that sober vision that hung around the bedrail.

He began a bitter conversation:

"Nurse, I'm only a ranker, but I had a bit saved. I went to a private doctor and paid for myself. And I went to a specialist, and he told me I should never get this. I paid for it myself out of what I had saved."

We might have been alone in the world, he and I. Far down at the other end of the room the men sat crouched about the fire, their trays before them on chairs. The sheet of window behind Mr. Wicks's head was flecked with the morsels of snow which, hunted by the gale, obtained a second's refuge before oblivion.

"I'd sooner be dead than lying here; I would, reely." You hear that often in the world. "I'd sooner be dead than——" But Mr. Wicks meant it; he would sooner be dead than lying there. And death is a horror, an end. Yet he says lying there is worse.

"You see, I paid for a specialist myself, and he told me I should never be like this."

There was nothing to be said. . . . One must have one's tea. I went down the ward to the bunk, and we cut the pink iced cake left over from Christmas. . . .

I did not mean to forget him, but I forgot

him. From birth to death we are alone. . . .

But one of the Sisters remembered him.

"Mr. Wicks is still in the dumps," she remarked.

"What is really the matter with him, Sister?"

"Locomotor ataxy." And she added as she drank her tea, "It's his own fault."

"Oh, hush, hush!" my heart cried soundlessly to her. "You can't judge the bitterness of this, nun, from your convent . . . !"

Alas, Mr. Wicks! . . . No wonder you saved your money to spend upon specialists! How many years have you walked in fear of this? He took your money, the gentleman in Harley Street, and told you that you might go in peace. He blessed you and gave you salvation.

And the bitterest thing of all is that you paid for him like an officer and he was wrong.

How the blinds blew and the windows shook to-night . . . ! I walked out of the hospital into a gale, clouds driving to the sea, trees bending back and fore across the moon.

I walked till I was warm, and then I walked for happiness.

The maddening shine of the moon held my eyes, and I walked in the road like a fool, watching her —till at last, bringing my eyes down, the telegraph-posts were small as blades of grass on the hill-side and the shining ribbon tracks in the mud on the road ran up the hill for ever. They go to Dover, and Dover is France—and France leads anywhere.

To what a lost enchantment am I recalled by the sight of a branch across the moon? Something in childhood, something which escapes yet does not wither. . . .

As I passed the public-house on the crest of the hill, all black and white in the cold moonlight, a heavy door swung open and, with a cough and a deep, satisfied snuffle, a man coming out let a stream of gas-light across the road. If I were a man I should certainly go to public-houses. All that polished brass and glass boxed up away from the moon and the shadows would call to me. And to drink must be a happy thing when you have climbed the hill.

The T.B. ward is a melancholy place. There is a man in a bed near the door who lies with his mouth open; his head is like a bird-cage beneath a muslin cloth; I saw him behind his screens when I took them over a little lukewarm chicken left from our dinner.

There was a dark red moon to-night, and frost. Our orderly said: "You can tell it's freezing, nurse, by the breath," as he watched mine curl up in smoke in the icy corridor. I like people who notice things. . . .

Out in the road in front of the hospital I couldn't

get the motor-bicycle to work, and sat crouched in the dark fiddling with spanners.

The charwomen came out of the big gate in the dark talking and laughing, all in a bunch. One of them stepped off the pavement near me and stopped to put her toe through the ice in the gutter.

"Nah, come on, Mrs. Toms!"

"I always 'ave to break it, it's ser nice an' stiff," she said as she ran after them.

To be a Sister is to have a nationality.

As there are Icelanders urbane, witty, lazy . . . and yet they are all Icelanders . . . so there are cold, uproarious, observant, subservient, slangy, sympathetic, indifferent, and Scotch Sisters, and yet . . .

Sister said of a patient to-day, "He was a funny man."

A funny man is a man who is a dark horse: who is neither friendly nor antagonistic; who is witty; who is preoccupied; who is whimsical or erratic— funny qualities, unsafe qualities.

No Sister could like a funny man.

In our ward there are three sorts of men: "Nothing much," "nice boys," and Mr. Wicks.

The last looms even to the mind of the Sister as a Biblical figure, a pillar of salt, a witness to God's wrath.

The Sister is a past-mistress of such phrases as: "Indeed!" "That is a matter of opinion," "We shall see . . ." "It is possible."

I have discovered a new and (for me) charming game which I play with my Sister. It is the game of telling the truth about the contents of my mind when asked.

Yesterday Sister was trying to get some coal out of the coal-bin with a shovel that turned round and round on its handle; she was unsuccessful.

I said: "Let me, Sister!"

She said: "Why?"

And I: "Because I think I can do it better."

"Why should you think that?"

"Because all human beings do," I said, and, luckily, she smiled.

She was washing her caps out in a bowl in the afternoon when I came on.

"Good afternoon, Sister," I said. "Ironing?"

"I am obviously only washing as yet," she said.

"It's because I think so quickly, Sister," I said; "I knew you would iron next."

I dined with Irene last night after the hospital.

I refused to believe what she told me about the last bus passing at half-past nine, and so at a quarter to ten I stood outside "The Green Lamp" and waited.

Ten minutes passed and no bus.

With me were two women waiting too—one holding a baby; the other, younger, smarter, dangling a purse.

At last I communicated my growing fears: "I believe the last has gone. . . ."

We fixed our six eyes on the far corner of the road, waiting for the yellow lights to round it, but only the gas-lamps stood firm in their perspective.

"Oh my, Elsie!" said the woman with the baby, "you can't never walk up to the cross-roads in the dark alone!"

"I wouldn't make the attempt, not for anything!" replied the younger one firmly.

Without waiting for more I stepped into the middle of the road and started on my walk home; the very next sentence would have suggested that Elsie and I should walk together.

She wouldn't "make the attempt . . ." Her words trailed through my mind, conjuring up some adventure, some act of bravery and daring.

The road was the high road, the channel of tarmac and pavements that she probably walked along every day; and now it was the selfsame high road, the same flagstones, hedges, railings, but with the cloak of night upon them.

It wasn't man she feared; even in the dark I knew she wasn't that kind. She would be awfully capable—with man. No, it was the darkness, the spooky jungle of darkness: she feared the trees would move. . . .

"I wouldn't make the attempt, not for anything"; and the other woman had quite agreed with her.

I knew where I was by the smells and the sounds on the road—the smell of the lines of picketed horses behind the railings, the sharp and sudden stamp of the sick ones in the wooden stables, and, later on, the glitter of water in the horse-troughs.

I thought: "I am not afraid. . . . Is it because I am more educated, or have less imagination?"

"Halt! Who goes there?"

"Friend," I said, thrilling tremendously.

He approached me and said something which I couldn't make anything of. Presently I disentangled, "You should never dread the baynit, miss."

"But I'm not dreading," I said, annoyed, "I . . . I love it."

He said he was cold, and added: "I bin wounded. If you come to that lamp you can see me stripe."

We went to the lamp. "It's them buses," he complained, "they won't stop when I halt 'em."

"But why do you want to stop them? They can't poison the horse-troughs."

"It's me duty," he said. "There's one comin'."

A bus, coming the opposite way, bore down upon us with an unwieldy rush and roar—the last bus, in a hurry to get to bed.

"You'll see," he said pessimistically.

" 'Alt! 'Alt, there!" The bus, with three

soldiers hanging on the step, rushed past us, and seemed to slow a little. The sentry ran a few paces towards it, crying " 'Alt!" But it gathered speed and boomed on again, buzzing away between the gas-lamps. He returned to me sadly.

"I don't believe they can hear," I said, and gave him some chocolates and went on.

As I passed the hospital gates it seemed there was a faint, a very faint, sweet smell of chloroform. . . .

I was down at the hospital to-night when the factory blew up over the river.

The lights went out, and as they sank I reached the kitchen hatchway with my tray. At the bottom of the stairs I could see through the garden door the sky grown sulphur and the bushes glowing, while all the panes of glass turned incandescent.

Then the explosion came; it sounded as though it was just behind the hospital. Two hundred panes of glass fell out, and they made a noise too.

Standing in the dark with a tray in my hand I heard a man's voice saying gleefully, "I haven't been out of bed this two months!"

Someone lit a candle, and by its light I saw all the charwomen from the kitchen bending about like broken weeds, and every officer was saying, "There, there now!"

We watched the fires till midnight from the hill.

I went over this morning early. We were thirty-two in a carriage—Lascars, Chinese, children, Jews, niggers from the docks.

Lascars and children and Jews and I, we fought to get off the station platform; sometimes there wasn't room on the ground for both my feet at once.

The fires were still burning and smouldering there at midday, but a shower of rime fell on it, so that it looked like an old ruin, something done long ago.

At Pompeii, someone told me, one looked into the rooms and they were as they had been left—tables laid. . . . Here, too, I saw a table laid for the evening meal with a bedstead fallen from the upper floor astraddle across it. The insides of the houses were coughed into their windows, basket-chairs hanging to the sills, and fire-irons.

Outside, the soil of the earth turned up; a workman's tin mug stuck and roasted and hardened into what looks like solid rock—a fossil, as though it had been there for ever.

London is only skin-deep. Beneath lies the body of the world.

The hump under the blankets rolls over and a man's solemn face appears upon the pillow.

"Can you get me a book, nurse?"

"Yes. What kind do you like?"

"Nothing fanciful; something that might be true."

"All right!"

"Oh—and nurse . . . ?"

"Yes?"

"Not sentimental and not funny. I like a practical story."

I got him "Lord Jim."

Another voice: "Nurse, is there any modern French poetry in that bookcase?"

"Good heavens, no! Who would have brought it here?"

(Who are they all . . . these men with their differing tastes?)

Perhaps the angels feel like this as they trail about in heaven with their wings flapping on their thin white legs. . . .

"Who were you, angel?"

"I was a beggar outside San Marco."

"Were you? How odd! I was an Englishman."

The concerts that we give in the ward touch me with some curious emotion. I think it is because I am for once at rest in the ward and have time to think and wonder.

There is Captain Thomson finishing his song. He doesn't know what to do with his hands; they swing. He is tall and dark, with soft eyes—and staff badges.

Could one guess what he is? Never in a

dozen years. . . . But *I know!*

He said to me last night, "Nurse, I'm going out to-morrow."

I leant across the table to listen to him.

"Nurse, if you ever want any *crêpe de Chine* . . . for nightgowns . . . mind, at wholesale prices . . ."

"I have bought some at a sale."

"May I ask at what price?"

"Four-and-eleven a yard."

"Pity! You could have had it from me at three!"

He gave me his business card. "That's it, nurse," he said, as he wrote on the back of it. "Drop me a line to that address and you'll get any material for underwear at trade prices."

He booked one or two orders the night he went away—not laughingly, not as a joke, but with deep seriousness, and gravely pleased that he was able to do what he could for us. He was a traveller in ladies' underwear. I have seldom met anyone so little a snob. . . .

Watch Mr. Gray singing. . . .

One hand on the piano, one on his hip:

"I love every mouse in that old-fashioned house."

"That fellow can sing!" whispers the man beside me.

"Is he a professional?" I asked as, finishing,

the singer made the faintest of bows and walked back to his chair.

"I think he must be."

"He is, he is!" whispered Mr. Matthews; "I've heard him before."

They know so little about each other, and they don't ask. It is only I who wonder—I, a woman, and therefore of the old, burnt-out world. These men watch without curiosity, speak no personalities, form no sets, express no likings, analyse nothing. They are new-born; they have as yet no standards and do not look for any.

Ah, to have had that experience too! . . . I am of the old world.

Again and again I realize, "A nation in arms. . . ."

Watchmakers, jewellers, station-masters, dressdesigners, actors, travellers in underwear, bank clerks . . . they come here in uniforms and we put them into pyjamas and nurse them; and they lie in bed or hobble about the ward, watching us as we move, accepting each other with the unquestioning faith of children.

The outside world has faded since I have been in the hospital. Their world is often near me— their mud and trenches, things they say when they come in wounded.

The worst of it is, it almost bores me to go to London, and London was always my Mecca. It is this garden at home, I think. It is so easy not to leave it.

When you wake up the window is full of branches, and last thing at night the moon is on the snow on the lawn and you can see the pheasants' footmarks.

Then one goes to the hospital. . . .

When Madeleine telephones to me, "I'm living in a whirl . . ." it disturbs me. Suddenly I want to, too, but it dies down again.

Not that it is their world, those trenches. When they come in wounded or sick they say at once, "What shows are on?"

Mr. Wicks has ceased to read those magazines his sister sends him; he now stares all day at his white bedrail.

I only pass him on my way to the towel-cupboard, twice an evening, and then as I glance at him I am set wondering all down the ward of what he thinks, or if he thinks. . . .

I may be quite wrong about him; it is possible he doesn't think at all, but stares himself into some happier dream.

One day when he is dead, when he is as totally dead as he tells me he hopes to be, that bed with its haunted bedrail will bend under another man's weight. Surely it must be haunted? The weight of thought, dream or nightmare, that hangs about it now is almost visible to me.

Mr. Wicks is an uneducated and ordinary man. In what manner does his dream run? Since he has ceased to read he has begun to drop away a little from my living understanding.

He reflects deeply at times.

To-night, as I went quickly past him with my load of bath-towels, his blind flapped a little, and I saw the moon, shaped like a horn, behind it.

Dropping my towels, I pulled his blind back:

"Mr. Wicks, look at the moon."

Obedient as one who receives an order, he reached up to his supporting handle and pulled his shoulders half round in bed to look with me through the pane.

The young moon, freed from the trees, was rising over the hill.

I dropped the blind again and took up my towels and left him.

After that he seemed to fall into one of his trances, and lay immovable an hour or more. When I took his dinner to him he lifted his large, sandy head and said:

"Seems a queer thing that if you hadn't said 'Look at the moon' I might have bin dead without seeing her."

"But don't you ever look out of the window?"

The obstinate man shook his head.

There was a long silence in the ward to-night. It was so cold that no one spoke. It is a gloomy ward, I think; the pink silk on the electric lights is so much too thick, and the fire smokes dreadfully. The patients sat round the fire with their "British warms" over their dressing-gowns and the collars turned up.

Through the two glass doors and over the landing you can see the T.B.'s moving like little cinema figures backwards and forwards across the lighted entrance.

Suddenly—a hesitating touch—an ancient polka struck up, a tune remembered at children's parties. Then a waltz, a very old one too. The T.B.'s were playing dance music.

I crept to their door and looked. One man alone was taking any notice, and he was the player; the others sat round coughing or staring at nothing in particular, and those in bed had their heads turned away from the music.

The man whose face is like a bird-cage has now more than ever a look of . . . an empty cage. He allows his mouth to hang open: that way the bird will fly.

What is there so rapturous about the moon?

The radiance of a floating moon is unbelievable. It is a figment of dream. The metal-silver ball that hung at the top of the Christmas tree, or, earlier still, the shining thing, necklace or spoon, the thing the baby leans to catch . . . the magpie in us . . .

Mr. Beecher is to be allowed to sleep till eight. He sleeps so badly, he says. He woke up crying this morning, for he has neurasthenia.

That is what Sister says.

He should have been in bed all yesterday, but instead he got up and through the door watched the dead T.B. ride away on his stretcher (for the bird flew in the night).

"How morbid of him!" Sister says.

He has seen many dead in France and snapped his fingers at them, but I agree with him that to die of tuberculosis in the backwaters of the war isn't the same thing.

It's dreary; he thought how dreary it was as he lay awake in the night.

But then he has neurasthenia. . . .

Pity is exhaustible. What a terrible discovery! If one ceases for one instant to pity Mr. Wicks he becomes an awful bore. Some days, when the sun is shining, I hear his grieving tenor voice all over the ward, his legendary tale of a wrong done him in his promotion. The men are kind to him and say "Old man," but Mr. Gray, who lies in the next bed to him, is drained of everything except resignation. I heard him say yesterday, "You told me that before. . . ."

We had a convoy last night.

There was a rumour at tea-time, and suddenly

I came round a corner on an orderly full of such definite information as:

"There's thirty officers, nurse; an 'undred an' eighty men."

I flew back to the bunk with the news, and we sat down to our tea wondering and discussing how many each ward would get.

Presently the haughty Sister from downstairs came to the door: she held her thin, white face high, and her rimless glasses gleamed, as she remarked, overcasually, after asking for a hot-water bottle that had been loaned to us:

"Have you many beds?"

"Have they many beds?" The one question that starts up among the competing wards.

And, "I don't want any; I've enough to do as it is!" is the false, cloaking answer that each Sister gives to the other.

But my Sisters are frank women; they laughed at my excitement—themselves not unstirred. It's so long since we've had a convoy.

The gallants of the ward showed annoyance. New men, new interests. . . . They drew together and played bridge.

A little flying boy with bright eyes said in his high, piping voice to me across the ward:

"So there are soldiers coming into the ward to-night!"

I paused, struck by his accusing eyes.

"What do you mean? Soldiers . . . ?"

"I mean men who have been to the front, nurse."

The gallants raised their eyebrows and grew uproarious.

The gallants have been saying unprofessional things to me, and I haven't minded. The convoy will arm me against them. "Soldiers are coming into the ward."

Eight o'clock, nine o'clock. . . . If only one could eat something! I took a sponge-finger out of a tin, resolving to pay it back out of my tea next day, and stole round to the dark corner near the German ward to eat it. The Germans were in bed; I could see two of them. At last, freed from their uniform, the dark blue with the scarlet soup-plates, they looked—how strange!—like other men.

One was asleep. The other, I met his eyes so close; but I was in the dark, and he under the light of a lamp.

I knew what was happening down at the station two miles away; I had been on station duty so often. The rickety country station lit by one large lamp; the thirteen waiting V.A.D.'s; the long wooden table loaded with mugs of every size; kettles boiling; the white clock ticking on; that frowsy booking clerk . . .

Then the sharp bell, the tramp of the stretcher-bearers through the station, and at last the two engines drawing gravely across the lighted doorway, and carriage windows filled with eager faces, other carriage windows with beds slung across them, a vast Red Cross, a chemist's shop, a theatre, more windows, more faces. . . .

The stretcher-men are lined up; the M.O. meets the M.O. with the train; the train Sisters drift in to the coffee-table.

"Here they come! Walkers first . . ."

The station entrance is full of men crowding in and taking the steaming mugs of tea and coffee; men on pickaback with bandaged feet; men with only a nose and one eye showing, with stumbling legs, bound arms. The station, for five minutes, is full of jokes and witticisms; then they pass out and into the waiting chars-à-bancs.

A long pause.

"Stretchers!"

The first stretchers are laid on the floor.

There I have stood so often, pouring the tea behind the table, watching that littered floor, the single gas-lamp ever revolving on its chain, turning the shadows about the room like a wheel—my mind filled with pictures, emptied of thoughts, hypnotized.

But last night, for the first time, I was in the ward. For the first time I should follow them

beyond the glass door, see what became of them,
how they changed from soldiers into patients. . . .

The gallants in the ward don't like a convoy; it
unsexes us.

Nine o'clock . . . ten o'clock. . . . Another
biscuit. Both Germans are asleep now.

At last a noise in the corridor, a tramp on the
stairs. . . . Only walkers? No, there's a stretcher
—and another . . . !

Now reflection ends, my feet begin to move, my
hands to undo bootlaces, flick down thermometers,
wash and fetch and carry.

The gallants play bridge without looking up. I
am tremendously fortified against them: for one
moment I fiercely condemn and then forget them.
For I am without convictions, antipathies,
prejudices, reflections. I only work and watch,
watch. . . .

Our ward is divided: half of it is neat and white
and orderly; the other half has khaki tumbled all
over it—"Sam Brownes," boots, caps, mud, the
caked mud from the "other side."

But the neat beds are empty; the occupants out
talking to the new-comers, asking questions.
Only the gallants play their bridge unmoved.
They are on their mettle, showing off. Their turn
will come some day.

Now it only remains to walk home, hungry,
under a heavy moon.

INSIDE THE GLASS DOORS

The snow is running down the gutters. What a strange and penetrating smell of spring! February . . . can it be yet?

The running snow is uncovering something that has been delayed. In the garden a blackbird made a sudden cry in the hedge. I did smell spring, and I'm starving. . . .

I thought last night that a hospital ward is, above all, a serene place, in spite of pain and blood and dressings. Gravity rules it and order and a quiet procession of duties.

Last night I made beds with the eldest Sister. The eldest Sister is good company to make beds with; she is quiet unless I rouse her, and when I talk she smiles with her eyes. I like to walk slowly round the ward, stooping and rising over the white beds, flicking the sheets mechanically from the mattress, and finally turning the mattress with an ease which gives me pleasure because I am strong.

In life nothing is too small to please. . . .

Once during the evening the eldest Sister said to me:

"I am worried about your throat. Is it no better?"

And from the pang of pleasure and gratitude that went through me I have learnt the value of such remarks.

In every bed there is someone whose throat

is at least more sore than mine. . . .

Though I am not one of those fierce V.A.D.'s who scoff at sore throats and look for wounds, yet I didn't know it was so easy to give pleasure.

The strange, disarming ways of men and women!

I stood in the bunk to-night beside the youngest Sister, and she looked up suddenly with her absent stare and said, "You're not so nice as you used to be!"

I was dumbfounded. Had I been "nice"? And now different. . . .

What a maddening sentence, for I felt she was going to refuse me any spoken explanation.

But one should not listen to what people say, only to what they mean, and she was one of those persons whose minds one must read for oneself, since her words so often deformed her thoughts.

The familiarity and equality of her tone seemed to come from some mood removed from the hospital, where her mistrustful mind was hovering about a trouble personal to herself.

She did not mean "You are not so nice . . ." but "You don't like me so much . . ."

She was so young, it was all so new to her, she wanted so to be "liked"! But there was this question of her authority. . . .

How was she to live among her fellows?

Can one afford to disdain them? Can one steer happily with indifference? Must one, to be "liked," bend one's spirit to theirs? And, most disturbing question of all, is to be "liked" the final standard?

Whether to wear, or not to wear, a mask towards one's world? For there is so much that is not ripe to show—change and uncertainty. . . .

As she sat there, unfolding to me the fogs of her situation, her fresh pink face clouded, her grand cap and red cape adding burdens of authority to the toil of growth, I could readily have looked into the glass to see if my hair was grey!

"Then there is nothing you condemn?" said the youngest Sister finally, at the close of a conversation.

I have to-day come up against the bedrock of her integrity; it is terrible. She has eternal youth, eternal fair hair, cold and ignorant judgments. On things relating to the world I can't further soften her; a man must do the rest.

"A gentleman . . . a gentleman . . ." I am so tired of this cry for a "gentleman."

Why can't they do very well with what they've got!

Here in the wards the Sisters have the stuff the world is made of laid out, bedded, before their eyes; the ups and downs of man from the four corners of the Empire and the hundred corners of social life, helpless and in pyjamas—and they're not satisfied, but must cry for a "gentleman"!

"I couldn't make a friend of that man!" the youngest Sister loves to add to her criticism of a patient.

It isn't my part as a V.A.D. to cry, "Who wants you to?"

"I couldn't trust that man!" the youngest Sister will say equally often.

This goes deeper. . . .

But whom need one trust? Brother, lover, friend . . . no more. Why wish to trust all the world? . . .

"They are not real men," she says, "not men through and through."

That's where she goes wrong; they are men through and through—patchy, ordinary, human. She means they are not men after her pattern.

Something will happen in the ward. Once I have touched this bedrock in her I shall be for ever touching it till it gets sore!

One should seek for no response. They are not elastic, these nuns. . . .

In all honesty the hospital is a convent, and the men in it my brothers.

This for months on end. . . .

For all that, now and then someone raises his eyes and looks at me; one day follows another and the glance deepens.

"Charme de l'amour qui pourrait vous peindre!"

Women are left behind when one goes into hospital. Such women as are in a hospital should be cool, gentle; anything else becomes a torment to the "prisoner."

For me, too, it is bad; it brings the world back into my eyes; duties are neglected, discomforts unobserved.

But there are things one doesn't fight.

"Charme de l'amour . . ." The ward is changed! The eldest Sister and the youngest Sister are my enemies; the patients are my enemies —even Mr. Wicks, who lies on his back with his large head turned fixedly my way to see how often I stop at the bed whose number is 11.

Last night he dared to say, "It's not like you, nurse, staying so much with that rowdy crew. . ." The gallants . . . I know! But one among them has grown quieter, and his bed is No. 11.

Even Mr. Wicks is my enemy.

He watches and guards. Who knows what he might say to the eldest Sister? He has nothing to do all day but watch and guard.

In the bunk at tea I sit among thoughts of my own. The Sisters are my enemies. . . .

I am alive, delirious, but not happy.

I am at anyone's mercy; I have lost thirty friends in a day. The thirty-first is in bed No. 11.

This is bad: hospital cannot shelter this life we

lead, No. 11 and I. He is a prisoner, and I have my honour, my responsibility towards him; he has come into this room to be cured, not tormented.

Even my hand must not meet his—no, not even in a careless touch, not even in its "duty"; or, if it does, what risk!

I am conspired against: it is not I who make his bed, hand him what he wishes; some accident defeats me every time.

Now that I come to think of it, it seems strange that the Sisters should be my enemies. Don't we deserve sympathy and pity, No. 11 and I? From women, too. . . .

Isn't there a charm hanging about us? Aren't we leading magic days? Do they feel it and dislike it? Why?

I feel that the little love we have created is a hare whose natural fate is to be run by every hound. But I don't see the reason.

We can't speak, No. 11 and I, only a whispered word or two that seems to shout itself into every ear. We don't know each other.

Last night it was stronger than I. I let him stand near me and talk. I saw the youngest Sister at the far end of the ward by the door, but I didn't move; she was watching. The moment I took my eyes from her I forgot her. . . . This is how one feels when one is desperate; that is how trouble comes.

Later, I stood down by the hatch waiting for the tray of fish, and as I stood there, the youngest Sister beside me, he came down, for he was up and dressed yesterday, and offered to carry the tray. For he is reckless, too. . . .

She told him to go back, and said to me, looking from her young, condemning eyes, "I suppose he thinks he can make up for being the cause of all the lateness to-night."

"Sister . . ." and then I stopped short. I hated her. Were we late? I looked at the other trays. We were not late; it was untrue. She had said that because she had had to wrap her barb in something and hadn't the courage to reprove me officially. I resented that and her air of equality. Since I am under her authority and agree to it, why dare she not use it?

As for me, I dared not speak to her all the evening. She would have no weapons against me. If I am to remember she is my Sister I must hold my hand over my mouth.

She would not speak to me, either. That was wrong of her: she is in authority, not I.

It is difficult for her because she is so young; but I have no room for sympathy.

At moments I forget her position and, burning with resentment, I reflect, " . . . this school-girl . . ."

To-day I walked down to the hospital thinking:

"I must be stronger. It is I who, in the inverted position of things, should be the stronger. He is being tortured, and he has no release. He cannot even be alone a moment."

But at the hospital gates I thought of nothing but that I should see him.

In the bunk sat the eldest Sister, writing in a book. It passed through my head that the two Sisters had probably "sat" on my affairs together. I wondered without interest what the other had told her. Putting on my cap, I walked into the ward.

Surely his bed had had a pink eiderdown!

I walked up the ward and looked at it; but I knew without need of a second glance what had happened.

His bed was made in the fashion in which we make an empty bed, a bed that waits for a new patient. His locker was empty and stood open, already scrubbed. I smiled as I noticed they hadn't even left me that to do.

No one volunteered a word of explanation, no one took the trouble to say he had gone.

These women. . . . I smiled again. Only the comic phrase rang in my head: "They've properly done me in! Properly done me in . . ."

I went downstairs and fetched the trays, and all the time the smile was on my lips. These women. . . . Somehow I had the better of the

Sister. It is better to be in the wrong than in the right.

His friends looked at me a little, but apparently he had left no message for me.

Later I learnt that he had been taken to another hospital at two, while I came on at three.

Once during the evening the eldest Sister mentioned vaguely, "So-and-so has gone."

And I said aloud, after a little reflection, "Yes . . . in the nick of time, Sister."

During the evening I realized that I should never see him again. It was here in this ward the thing had grown. The hare we had started wouldn't bear the strain of any other life. He might write, but I shouldn't go and see him.

"He must be wild," I thought with pity.

The feeling between us would die anyhow; better throw in my strength with the Sister's and help her hurl it now towards its death. I looked at her bent head with a secret triumph.

Then, slowly: "How . . . permanently am I in disgrace?"

And she: "Not at all . . . now."

Behind the stone pillar of the gateway is one dirty little patch of snow; I saw it even in the moonless darkness.

The crown of the hill here holds the last snows, but for all that the spring smell is steaming among the trees and up and down the bracken slopes in the garden next door.

There is no moon, there are no stars, no promise to the eye, but in the dense, vapouring darkness the bulbs are moving. I can smell what is not earth or rain or bark.

The curtain has been drawn over No. 11; the Sister holds the corners tightly against the window-frame. He is outside, somewhere in the world, and I am here moving among my thirty friends; and since it isn't spring yet, the lights are lit to hide the twilight. The Sister's eyes talk to me again as we make beds—yes, even bed No. 11 with a little jaundice boy in it. They let me make it now!

Last night we had another concert in the ward.

A concert demoralizes me. By reason of sitting on the beds and talking to whom one wills, I regain my old manners, and forget that a patient may be washed, fed, dressed but not talked to. My old manners were more gracious, but less docile.

Afterwards we wheeled the beds back into their positions. I bumped Mr. Lambert's as I wheeled it, and apologized.

"I'm not grumbling," he smiled from his pillow.

"You never do," I answered.

"You don't know me, nurse!"

And I thought as I looked down at him, "I shall

74

never know him better or so well again . . ."

Indeed a Sister is a curious creature. She is like a fortress, unassailable, and whose sleeping guns may fire at any minute.

I was struck with a bit of knowledge last night that will serve me through life, i.e., that to justify oneself is the inexcusable fault. It is better to be in the wrong than in the right.

A Sister has an "intimate life."

It occurs when she goes off duty; that is to say, it lies between 8.45, when she finishes her supper, and 10 o'clock, when she finishes undressing.

That is why one Sister said to me, "If I hadn't taken up nursing I should have gone in for culture."

I don't laugh at that. . . . To have an intimate life one must have a little time.

Who am I that I can step in from outside to criticize? The hospital is not my life. I am expectant. . . .

But for them here and now is the business of life.

As the weeks go by I recognize the difficulty of keeping the life of the Sisters and the V.A.D.'s out of the circle of my thoughts. Their vigorous and symmetrical vision of the ward attacks me; their attitude towards the patients, which began by offending me, ends by overtaking me.

On the whole the Sisters loathe relations. They look into the ward and see the mothers and sisters and wives camped round the beds, and go back into the bunk feeling that the ward doesn't belong to them.

The eldest Sister said to me yesterday: "Shut the door, nurse; there's Captain Fellows's father. I don't want him fussing round."

On that we discussed relations, and it seemed to me that it was inevitable that a Sister should be the only buffer between them and their pressing anxieties.

"No, a relation is the last straw. . . . You don't understand!" she said.

I don't understand; but I am not specialized.

Long ago in the Mess I said to *my* Sister, laughing: "I would go through the four years' training just to wear that cap and cape!"

And she: "You couldn't go through it and come out as you are . . ."

Mr. Wicks has set his heart on crutches.

"If you won't try me on them I'll buy me own and walk out of here!"

Then I realize the vanity of his threat and the completeness of his imprisonment, and hurry to suggest a new idea before he sees it too. . . .

We set him on crutches. . . .

He is brave. He said with anger: "I can't

stand on these, they're too long. You go and ask for some shorter ones . . ."

And thus together we slurred over the fact of that pendulous, nerveless body which had hung from the crutches like an old stocking.

But all the evening he was buried in his own silence, and I suppose he was looking at the vision on the bedrail.

A boy of seventeen was brought in yesterday with pneumonia.

He was so ill that he couldn't speak, and we put screens round his bed. All the other patients in the ward immediately became convalescents.

I helped Sister to wash him, holding him on his side while he groaned with pain; and Sister, no longer cynical: said, "There you are, Sonnie, it's almost finished . . ."

When I rolled back the blanket it gave me a shock to see how young his feet were—clean and thin, with the big toe curling up and the little toes curling back.

"Will you brush my hair?" he managed to say to me, and when I had finished: "This is a pretty ward . . ."

It isn't, but I am glad it seems so to him.

The boy is at his worst. Whenever we come near him he lifts his eyes and asks, "What are you going to do now?"

But to whatever we do he submits with a terrible docility.

Lying there propped on his pillow, with his small yellow face staring down the ward, he is all the centre of my thoughts; I am preoccupied with the mystery that is in his lungs.

Five days ago he was walking on his legs: five days, and he is on the edge of the world—to-night looking over the edge.

There is no shell, no mark, no tear. . . . The attack comes from within.

The others in the ward are like phantoms.

When I say to-morrow, "How is the boy?" what will they say?

The sun on the cobwebs lights them as it lights the telephone-wires above. The cocks scream from every garden.

To-day the sky is like a pale egg-shell, and aeroplanes from the two aerodromes are droning round the hill.

I think from time to time, "Is he alive?"

Can one grow used to death? It is unsafe to think of this. . . .

For if death becomes cheap it is the watcher, not the dying, who is poisoned.

His mother buys a cake every day and brings it at tea-time, saying, "For the Sisters' tea. . . ."

It is a bribe, dumbly offered, more to be on the safe side of every bit of chance than because she really believes it can make the slightest difference.

Now that I have time to think of it, her little action hurts me, but yesterday I helped to eat it with pleasure because one is hungry and the margarine not the best.

Aches and pains. . . .
      Pains and aches. . . .

I don't know how to get home up the long hill. . . .

Measles. . . .

(Unposted.)

"DEAR SISTER,—Four more days before they will let me out of bed. . . . Whatever I promise to a patient in future I shall do, if I have to wear a notebook hanging on my belt.

"By which you will see that I am making discoveries!

"The quality of *expectation* in a person lying horizontally is wrought up to a high pitch. One is always expecting something. Generally it is food; three times a day it is the post; oftener it is the performance of some promise. The things that one asks from one's bed are so small: 'Can you get me a book?' 'Can you move that vase of flowers?' 'When you come up next time could you bring me an envelope?'

"But if one cannot get them life might as well stop.

"The wonder to me is how they stood me!

"I was always cheerful—I thought it a merit; I find instead it is an exasperation.

"I make a hundred reflections since my eyes are too bad to read. I stare at the ceiling, and if a moth comes on it—and just now that happened, or I would not have thought of mentioning it—I watch the pair of them, the moth and its leaping shadow, as they whirl from square to square of the smoke-ripened ceiling. This keeps my thoughts quiet.

"Then in the daytime there is the garden, the dog that crosses the lawn, the gardener talking to himself, the girl who goes to feed the hens. . . .

"I don't say that in any of these things I find a substitute for reading, but since I can't and mayn't read . . .

"I am thinking, you know, of the beds down the right-hand side of the ward.

"There's Mr. Wicks, now: he has his back to the road with the trams on it.

"Do you see anything in that?

"I do. But then I have the advantage of you; my position is horizontal.

"Mr. Wicks's position is also . . . strictly . . .

horizontal. It seems to me that if he could see those trams, mark Saturdays and Sundays by the increase of passengers, make little games to himself involving the number of persons to get on and off (for the stopping-place is within view: I know, for I looked) it might be possible to draw him back from that apathy which I too, as well as you, was ceasing to notice.

"Mr. Wicks, Sister, not only has his back to the road with trams on it, but for eleven months he has had his eyes on the yellow stone of the wall of the German ward; that is, when they are not on his own bedrail. . . .

"But if his bed were turned round to range alongside the window . . . ? For he is a man with two eyes; not one who can write upon a stone wall with his thoughts.

"And yet . . . it would be impossible! There's not a ward in the hospital whose symmetry is so spoilt.

"And that, you know, is a difficulty for you to weigh. How far are you a dictator?

"I have been thinking of my rôle and yours.

"In the long run, however 'capable' I become, my soul should be given to the smoothing of pillows.

"You are barred from so many kinds of sympathy: you must not sympathize over the deficiencies of the hospital, over the food, over the

M.O.'s lack of imagination, over the intolerable habits of the man in the next bed; you must not sigh 'I know . . .' to any of these plaints.

"Yours is the running of the ward. Yours the isolation of a crowned head.

"One day you said a penetrating thing to me:

" 'He's not very ill, but he's feeling wretched. Run along and do the sympathetic V.A.D. touch!'

"For a moment I, just able to do a poultice or a fomentation, resented it.

"But you were right. . . . One has one's *métier*."

III

"THE BOYS . . ."

III

"THE BOYS . . ."

So now one steps down from chintz covers and lemonade to the Main Army and lemon-water.

And to show how little one has one's eye upon the larger issues, the thing that upset me most on coming into a "Tommies'" ward was the fact that instead of twenty-six lemons twice a day for the making of lemonade I now squeeze two into an old jug and hope for the best about the sugar.

Smiff said to-day, "Give us a drop of lemon, nurse . . ." And the Sister: "Go on with you! I won't have the new nurse making a pet of you. . ."

I suppose I'm new to it, and one can't carry on the work that way, but, God knows, the water one can add to a lemon is cheap enough!

Smiff had a flash of temper to-night. He said: "Keepin' me here starin' at green walls this way! Nothing but green, nine blessed months!"

His foot is off, and to-night for the first time the doctor had promised that he should be wheeled into the corridor. But it was forgotten, and I am too new to jog the memory of the gods.

It's a queer place, a "Tommies'" ward. It makes me nervous. I'm not simple enough; they make me shy. I can't think of them like the others do, as "the boys"; they seem to me full-grown men.

I suffer awfully from my language in this ward. I seem to be the only V.A.D. of whom they continually ask, "What say, nurse?" It isn't that I use long words, but my sentences seem to be inverted.

An opportunity for learning to speak simple Saxon. . . .

"An antitetanic injection for Corrigan," said Sister. And I went to the dispensary to fetch the syringe and the needles.

"But has he any symptoms?" I asked. (In a Tommies' ward one dare ask anything; there isn't that mystery which used to surround the officers' illnesses.)

"Oh no," she said, "it's just that he hasn't had his full amount in France."

So I hunted up the spirit-lamp and we prepared it, talking of it.

But we forgot to talk of it to Corrigan. The needle was into his shoulder before he knew why his shirt was held up.

His wrath came like an avalanche; the discipline of two years was forgotten, his Irish tongue was loosened. Sister shrugged her shoulders and laughed; I listened to him as I cleaned the syringe.

I gathered that it was the indignity that had shocked his sense of individual pride. "Treating me like a cow . . ." I heard him say to Smiff—who laughed, since it wasn't his shoulder that carried the serum. Smiff laughed: he has been in hospital nine months, and his theory is that a Sister may do anything at any moment; his theory is that nothing does any good—that if you don't fuss you don't get worse.

Corrigan was angry all day; the idea that "a bloomin' woman should come an' shove something into me systim" was too much for him. But he forgets himself: there are no individualists now; his "system" belongs to us.

Sister said, laughing, to Smiff the other day, "Your leg is mine."

"Wrong again; it's the Governmint's!" said Smiff. But Corrigan is Irish and doesn't like that joke.

There are times when my heart fails me; when my eyes, my ears, my tongue, and my understanding fail me; when pain means nothing to me. . . .

In the bus yesterday I came down from London sitting beside a Sister from another ward, who held her hand to her ear and shifted in her seat.

She told me she had earache, and I felt sorry for her.

As she had earache we didn't talk, and I sat

huddled in my corner and watched the names of the shops, thinking, as I was more or less forced to do by her movements, of her earache.

What struck me was her own angry bewilderment before the fact of her pain. "But it hurts. . . . You've no idea how it hurts!" She was surprised.

Many times a day she hears the words, "Sister, you're hurtin' me. . . . Couldn't you shift my heel? It's like a toothache," and similar sentences. I hear them in our ward all the time. One can't pass down the ward without some such request falling on one's ears.

She is astonished at her earache; she is astonished at what pain can be; it is unexpected. She is ready to be angry with herself, with her pain, with her ear. It is monstrous, she thinks. . . .

The pain of one creature cannot continue to have a meaning for another. It is almost impossible to nurse a man well whose pain you do not imagine. A deadlock!

One has illuminations all the time!

There is an old lady who visits in our ward, at whom, for one or two unimportant reasons, it is the custom to laugh. The men, who fall in with our moods with a docility which I am beginning to suspect is a mask, admit too that she is comic.

This afternoon, when she was sitting by Corrigan's bed and talking to him I saw where her treatment of him differed from ours. She treats him as though he were an individual; but there is more in it than that. . . . She treats him as though he had a wife and children, a house and a back garden and responsibilities: in some manner she treats him as though he had dignity.

I thought of yesterday's injection. That is the difference: that is what the Sisters mean when they say "the boys." . . .

The story of Rees is not yet ended in either of the two ways in which stories end in a hospital. His arm does not get worse, but his courage is ebbing. This morning I wheeled him out to the awful sleep again—for the third time.

They will take nearly anything from each other. The only thing that cheered Rees up as he was wheeled away was the voice of Pinker crying, "Jer want white flowers on yer coffin? We'll see to the brass 'andles!"

From Pinker, a little boy from the Mile End Road, they will stand anything. He is the servant of the ward (he says), partly through his good nature and a little because he has two good arms and legs. "I ain't no skivvy," he protests all the time, but every little odd job gets done.

Rees, when he wakes, wakes sobbing and says, "Don' go away, nurse . . ." He holds my hand in a fierce clutch, then releases it to point in the air, crying, "There's the pain!" as though the pain filled the air and rose to the rafters. As he wakes it centralizes, until at last comes the moment when he says, "Me arm aches cruel," and points to it. Then one can leave him.

It was the first time I had heard a man sing at his dressing. I was standing at the sterilizer when Rees's song began to mount over the screen that hid him from me. ("Whatever is that?" "Rees's tubes going in.")

It was like this: "Ah . . . ee . . . oo, Sister!" and again: "Sister . . . oo . . . ee . . . ah!" Then a little scream and his song again.

I heard her voice: "Now then, Rees, I don't call that much of a song." She called me to make his bed, and I saw his left ear was full of tears.

O visitors, who come into the ward in the calm of the long afternoon, when the beds are neat and clean and the flowers out on the tables and the V.A.D.'s sit sewing at splints and sandbags, when the men look like men again and smoke and talk and read . . . if you could see what lies beneath the dressings!

When one shoots at a wooden figure it makes a hole. When one shoots at a man it makes a hole, and the doctor must make seven others.

I heard a backbird sing in the middle of the night last night—two bars, and then another. I thought at first it might be a burglar whistling to his mate in the black and rustling garden.

But it was a blackbird in a nightmare.

Those distant guns again to-night. . . .
Now a lull and now a bombardment; again a lull,
and then batter, batter, and the windows tremble.
Is the lull when *they* go over the top?

I can only think of death to-night. I tried to
think just now, "What is it, after all! Death
comes anyway; this only hastens it." But that
won't do; no philosophy helps the pain of death.
It is pity, pity, pity, that I feel, and sometimes a
sort of shame that I am here to write at all.

Summer. . . . Can it be summer through
whose hot air the guns shake and tremble? The
honeysuckle, whose little stalks twinkled and
shone that January night, has broken at each
woody end into its crumbled flower.

Where is the frost, the snow? . . . Where are
the dead?

Where is my trouble and my longing, and the
other troubles, and the happiness in other summers?

Alas, the long history of life! There is that in
death that makes the throat contract and the
heart catch: everything is written in water.

We talk of tablets to the dead. There can be
none but in the heart, and the heart fades.

There are only ten men left in bed in the ward.
Sometimes I think, "Will there never be another
convoy?"

91

And then: "Is not one man alone sufficient matter on which to reflect?" "One can find God in a herring's head . . ." says a Japanese proverb.

When there is not much to do in the ward and no sound comes from behind the screens, when there has not been a convoy for weeks, when the little rubber tubes lie in the trolley-drawer and the syringe gives place to the dry dressing—then they set one of us aside from the work of the ward to sit at a table and pad splints.

It isn't supposed to be a job we care for, and I am keeping up the delusion, but all the time I run my seams straight, pull the horsehair out to the last fine shred, turn in my corners as the corners of a leather book are turned, so that I may be kept at it, although out of cunning I appear to grumble and long to be released.

One does not wash up when one makes splints, one does not change the pillow-cases—forcing the resentful pillow down, down till the corners of the case are filled—nor walk the ward in search of odd jobs.

But these are not the reasons. . . .

Just as I liked the unending laying of the trays in the corridor, so making splints appears to me a gentle work in which one has time to look at and listen to the ward with more penetrating eyes, with wider ears—a work varied by long conversations with Pinker about his girl and the fountain-pen trade.

But I ought not to have asked if she were pretty.

At first he didn't answer and appeared to be thinking very seriously—of a way out, perhaps.

"Does fer me all right," he presently said.

The defence of his girl occupied his attention, for after a few minutes he returned to it: "Sensible sort of girl. She ain't soft. Can cook an' all that."

I went on sewing my splint.

Almost reluctantly he pursued: "Got 'er photograph 'ere." But he did not get up at once, and we turned to the fountain-pens. "Any nib," he said, "crossed ever so, *I* could mend it. Kep' the books too; we was always stocktaking."

Now I think of it, fountain-pen shops always *are* stocktaking. They do it all down the Strand, with big red labels across the front.

He rose suddenly and crossed to his locker to look for her photograph, returning after a few minutes with a bundle of little cardboards. The first I turned over was that of a pretty fair-haired girl. "Is that her?" I asked. "She's pretty!" "That's 'er young sister," he answered. I turned over the rest, and he pointed out his family one by one—last of all his girl.

There are some men who are not taken in by a bit of fair hair.

One knows what these cheap photographs are, how they distort and blacken. The girl who looked at me from this one appeared to be a monster.

She had an enormous face, enormous spectacles, bands of galvanized iron drawn across her forehead for hair. . . .

"Ther's just them two, 'er an' 'er sister. 'Er sister ain't got a feller yet."

I praised his girl to Pinker, and praised Pinker to myself.

"A girl friend," he said, "keeps yer straighter than a man. Makes yer punctual."

"So she won't wait for you when you are late?"

"Not a minute over time," he said with pride. "I used to be a terror when I first knew 'er; kep' 'er waitin' abaht. She soon cured me, did F. Steel."

"You are a funny little bird, Pinker," said the Sister, passing.

"Li'l bird, am I?" He tucked his cardboards carefully into his locker and followed her up the ward firing repartee.

I sewed my splint. In all walks of life men keep one waiting. I should like to ask the huge and terrible girl about her cure.

Monk is the ugliest man I have ever seen. He has a squint and a leer, his mouth drops at both sides, he has no forehead, and his straight, combed hair meets his eyebrows—or rather, his left eyebrow, since that one is raised by a cut. He has the expression of a cut-throat, and yet he is quite young, good-tempered, and shy.

When Monk was working at a woollen belt Pinker said: "Workin' that for yer girl? . . . You got a girl, Monk?"

Monk squinted sidelong at Pinker and rubbed his hands together like a large ape.

" 'E ain't got no girl," shrilled Pinker. "Monk ain't got no girl. You don' know what a girl is, do yer, Monk?"

Although they do much more to help each other than I ever saw done in the officers' ward, yet one is always saying things that I find myself praying the other hasn't heard.

In the next bed to Monk lies Gayner, six foot two, of the Expeditionary Force. Wounded at Mons, he was brought home to England, and since then he has made the round of the hospitals. He is a good-looking, sullen man who will not read or write or sew, who will not play draughts or cards or speak to his neighbour. He sits up, attentive, while the ulcers on his leg are being dressed, but if one asks him something of the history of his wound his tone holds such a volume of bitterness and exasperation that one feels that at any moment the locks of his spirit might cease to hold.

" . . . ever since Mons, these ulcers, on and off?"

"Yes."

"Oh well, we must cure them now."

Her light tone is what he cannot endure. He does not believe in cure and will not believe in cure.

It has become an article of faith: his ulcers will never be cured. He has a silent scorn of hospitals. He can wind a perfect bandage and he knows the rules; beyond that he pays as little attention as possible to what goes on.

When his dressing is over he tilts his thin, intelligent face at the ceiling. "Don't you ever read?" I asked him.

"I haven't the patience," he replied. But he has the patience to lie like that with his thin lips compressed and a frown on his face for hours, for days . . . since Mons. . . .

I have come to the conclusion that he has a violent soul, that he dare not talk. It is no life for a man.

I said to Pinker this morning, "I wish you'd hurry up over your bath; I've got to get it scrubbed out by nine."

"Don't you hurry me, nurse," said Pinker, "it's the on'y time I can think, in me bath."

I should like to have parried with Pinker (only my language is so much more complicated than it ought to be) that thinking in one's bath is a self-deception. I lay in my own bath last night and thought very deep thoughts, but often when we think our thoughts are deep they are only vague. Bath thoughts are wonderful, but there's nothing "to" them.

We had a heated discussion to-day as to whether the old lady who leaves a tract beneath a single rose by each bedside could longer be tolerated.

"She is a nuisance," said the Sister; "the men make more noise afterwards because they set her hymns to ragtime."

"What good does it do them?" said the V.A.D., " . . . and I have to put the roses in water!"

I rode the highest horse of all: "Her inquiries about their souls are an impertinence. Why should they be bothered?"

These are the sort of things they say in debating societies. But Life talks differently. . . .

Pinker said, "Makes the po'r ole lady 'appy!"

As one bends one's head low over the splint one sits unnoticed, a part of the furniture of the ward. The sounds of the ward rise and fill the ears; it is like listening to a kettle humming, bees round a bush of flowers, the ticking of a clock, the passing of life. . . .

Now and then there are incidents, as just now. Two orderlies came in with a stretcher to fetch Mr. Smith (an older man than Smiff and a more dignified) away to a convalescent home. Mr. Smith has never been to France, but walked into our ward one day with a sore on his foot which had to be cut. He was up and dressed in his bedraggled khaki uniform when the stretcher-bearers came for him.

He looked down his nose at the stretcher. "I don't much like the look of that," he said. The stretcher-bearers waited for him.

He stood irresolute. "I never bin in one of them, and I don't want to make a start."

"It's bad luck to be our name," called out Smiff, waving his amputated ankle. "Better get your hand in!"

Mr. Smith got in slowly and departed from the ward, sitting bolt upright, gripping the sides with his hands.

Some of the wards and the Sisters' bunks are charming at this time of the year, now that larkspur and rambler-roses are cheap in the market.

But the love of decoration is not woman's alone. Through the dispensary hatchway I saw three empty poison-bottles, each with a poppy stuck in its neck.

Everything in the dispensary is beautiful—its glasses, its flames, its brass weights, its jars and globes; but much more beautiful because it is half a floor higher than the corridor in which we stand and look up into it, through a hatchway in the wall. There is something in that: one feels like Gulliver.

No woman has ever been into this bachelors' temple.

On tapping at a small square panel set in the wall of the corridor the panel flies up and a bachelor is seen from the waist to the knees. If he feels well and my smile is humble he will stoop, and I see looking down at me a small worn face and bushy eyebrows, or a long ascetic face and bleached hair, or a beard and a pair of bearded nostrils.

Between them the three old things, priests in their way, measure and weigh and mix and scold and let up the panel and bang it down through the long day, filling the hospital with their coloured bottles, sealed packets of pills, jars and vaccines, and precious syringes in boxes marked "To be returned at once" (I never knew a Sister fail to toss her head when she saw this message).

It is a very social spot outside the panel of the dispensary: each V.A.D. goes there each morning as one might do one's marketing, and, meeting there, puts down her straw basket, taps at the panel, and listens to the scolding of the old men with only half an ear.

For the bachelors amuse themselves when they are not mixing and weighing by inventing odd rules and codes of their own, and, reaching a skinny arm through the hatchway, they pin them on, little scraps of paper which fall down and are swept to heaven in the charwomen's pails.

And the V.A.D.'s, who are not at all afraid, because one cannot be afraid of a man of whom one has never seen more than half, turn a blind eye to the slips and a deaf ear to the voices, bringing their bottles and their jars just in the manner they were taught to do when first they entered the hospital. And they gossip! They have just seen the morning papers on all the beds; they have just heard about the half-days for the week; they have collected little rags and ends of news as they came along the corridor.

They gossip. And once a bearded bachelor thumped the panel down almost on my finger, leaving three startled faces staring at a piece of painted wood. But a little dark girl worked the panel up an inch with her nails and cajoled through the crack.

I have said before that the long corridor is wonderful. In the winter afternoons and evenings, when the mist rolled up and down over the tiles like the smoke in a tunnel, when one walked almost in darkness and peered into the then forbidden wards, when dwarfs coming from the G block grew larger and larger till the A block turned them into beings of one's own size, the corridor always made a special impression on me.

But in the summer mornings it is remarkable too. Then regiments of charwomen occupy it, working in close mass formation. Seven will work abreast upon their knees, flanked by their pails, their hands moving backwards and forwards in so complicated a system that there appears to be no system at all.

Patches of the corridor are thick with soapsuds; patches are dry. The art of walking the corridor in the morning can be learnt, and for a year and five months I have done it with no more than a slip and a slide.

But yesterday I stepped on a charwoman's hand. It was worse than stepping on a puppy: one knows that sickening lift of the heart, as though the will could undo the weight of the foot. . . .

The stagger, the sense of one's unpardonable heaviness. . . . I slipped on her hand as on a piece of orange-peel, and, jumping like a chamois, sent the next pail all over the heels of the front rank.

It was the sort of situation with which one can do nothing.

I met a friend yesterday, one of the old Chelsea people. He has followed his natural development. Although he talks war, war, war, it is from his old angle, it wears the old hall-mark.

He belongs to a movement which believes it "feels the war." Personal injury or personal loss does not enter the question; the heart of this movement of his bleeds perpetually, but impersonally. He claims for it that this heart is able to bleed more profusely than any other heart, ndividual or collective, in . . . let us limit it to England!

In fact it is the only blood he has noticed.

When the taxes go up he says, "Well, now perhaps it will make people feel the war!" For he longs that every one should lose their money so that at last they may "feel the war," "stop the war" (interchangeable!).

He forgets that even in England a great many quite stupid people would rather lose their money than their sons.

How strange that these people should still picture the minds of soldiers as filled with the glitter of bright bayonets and the glory of war! They think we need a vision of blood and ravage and death to turn us from our bright thoughts, to still the noise of the drum in our ears. The drums don't beat, the flags don't fly. . . .

He should come down the left-hand side of the ward and hear what the dairyman says.

"I 'ates it, nurse; I 'ates it. Them 'orses'll kill me; them drills. . . . It's no life for a man, nurse."

The dairyman hasn't been to the Front; you needn't go to the Front to hate the war. Sometimes I get a glimpse from him of what it means to the weaklings, the last-joined, feeble creatures.

"Me 'ead's that queer, nurse; it seems to get queerer every day. I can't 'elp worryin'. I keep thinkin' of them 'orses."

Always the horses. . . .

I said to Sister, "Is No. 24 really ill?"

"There's a chance of his being mental," she said. "He is being watched."

Was he mental before the war took him, before the sergeant used to whip the horses as they got to the jumps, before the sergeant cried out, "Cross your stirrups!"?

It isn't his fault; there are strong and feeble men.

A dairyman's is a gentle job; he could have scraped through life all right. He sleeps in the afternoon, and stirs and murmurs: "Drop your reins. . . . Them 'orses, sergeant! I'm comin', sergeant; don't touch 'im this time!" And then in a shriller voice, "Don't touch 'im . . ." Then he wakes.

Poor mass of nerves. . . . He nods and smiles every time one looks at him, frantic to please.

There are men and men. Scutts has eleven wounds, but he doesn't "mind" the war. God made many brands of men, that is all; one must accept them.

But war finds few excuses; and there are strange minnows in the fishing-net. Sometimes, looking into the T.B. ward, I think: "It almost comes to this: one must spit blood or fight . . ."

"Why don't you refuse?" my friend would say to the dairyman. "Why should you fight because another man tells you to?"

It isn't so simple as that, is it, dairyman? It isn't even a question of the immense, vague machinery behind the sergeant, but just the sergeant himself: it isn't a question of generals or politicians, of great wrongs or fierce beliefs . . . but of the bugle which calls you in the morning and the bugle which puts you to bed at night.

Well, well. . . . The dairyman is in hospital, and that is the best that he can hope for.

I read a book once about a prison. They too, the prisoners, sought after the prison hospital, as one seeks after one's heaven.

It is so puffed up of my friend to think that his and his "movement's" are the only eyes to see the vision of horror. Why, these others *are* the vision!

This afternoon I was put at splints again.

I only had an inch or two to finish and I spun it out, very happy.

Presently the foot of a bed near me began to catch my attention: the toe beneath the sheets became more and more agitated, then the toes of the other foot joined the first foot, beating a frenzied tattoo beneath the coverings. I looked up.

Facing me a pair of blue eyes were bulging above an open mouth, the nostrils were quivering, the fingers were wrung together. It was Gayner surely seeing a ghost.

I rose and went to his bed.

"My jaws want to close," he muttered. "I can't keep them open."

I jumped and went for Sister, who took the news in a leisurely fashion, which reproved me for my excitement. Feeling a fool, I went and sat down again, taking up my splint. But there was no forgetting Gayner.

I tried to keep my eyes on my work, but first his toes and then his hands filled all my mind, till at last I had to look up and meet the eyes again.

Still looking as though he had seen a ghost—a beast of a ghost . . .! In hospital since Mons. . . . "I wonder how many men he has seen die of tetanus?" I thought.

"He's got the jumps," I thought.

So had I. Suppose Sister was wrong! Suppose the precious minutes were passing! Suppose . . .! She was only the junior Sister.

"Shall I get you some water?" I said at last. He nodded, and gulped in a horrible fashion. I got him the mug, and while he drank I longed, but did not dare, to say, "Are you afraid of . . . that?" I thought if one could say the word it might break down that dumb fright, draw the flesh up again over those bulging eyes, give him a sort of anchor, a confessional, even if it was only me. But I didn't dare. Gayner is one of those men so pent up, so rigid with some inner indignation, one cannot tamper with the locks.

Again I went and sat down.

When next I looked up he was sweating. He beckoned to me: "Ask Sister to send for the doctor. I can't stand this."

I went and asked her.

She sucked her little finger thoughtfully. "Give him the thermometer," she said. He couldn't take it in his mouth, " . . . for if I shut my lips they'll never open." I put it under his arm and waited while his feet kicked and his hands twisted. He was normal. Sister smiled.

But by a coincidence the doctor came, gimlet-eyed.

"Hysteria . . ." he said to Sister in the bunk.

"Is no one going to reassure Gayner?" I wondered. And no one did.

Isn't the fear of pain next brother to pain itself? Tetanus or the fear of tetanus—a choice between two nightmares. Don't they admit that?

So, forbidden to speak to him, I finished my splint till tea-time. But I couldn't bring myself to sit down to it, for fear that the too placid resumption of my duties should outrage him. I stood up.

Which helped me, not him.

After the dressings are over we scrub the dishes and basins in the annexe.

In the annexe, except that there is nothing to sit on, there is leisure and an invitation to reflection.

Beneath the windows legions of white butterflies attack the cabbage-patch which divides us from the road; beyond the road there is a camp from which the dust flows all day.

When the wind is from the north the dust is worse than ever and breaks like a surf over the cabbages, while the butterflies try to rise above it; but they never succeed, and dimly one can see the white wings beating in the whirlpool.

I shall never look at white butterflies again without hearing the sounds from the camp, without seeing the ring of riders, without thinking perhaps, of the dairyman and of the other "dairymen."

The butterflies do not care for noise. When, standing beside the cabbage-patch, the bugler blows the dinner-bugle, they race in a cloud to the far corner and hover there until the last note is sounded.

I think it is I who am wrong when I consider the men as citizens, as persons of responsibility, and the Sister right when she says "the boys."

Taken from their women, from their establishments, as monks or boys or even sheep are housed, they do not want, perhaps, to be reminded of an existence to which they cannot return; until a limb is off, or the war ends.

To what a point they leave their private lives behind them! To what a point their lives are suspended. . . .

On the whole, I find that in hospital they do not think of the future or of the past, nor think much at all. As far as life and growth goes it is a hold-up!

There is really not much to hope for; the leave is so short, the home-life so disrupted that it cannot be taken up with content. Perhaps it isn't possible to let one's thoughts play round a life about which one can make no plans.

They are adaptable, living for the minute—their present hope for the cup of tea, for the visiting day, for the concert; their future hope for the drying of the wound, for the day when the Sister's fingers may press, but no drop be wrung from the long scar.

Isn't it curious to wish so passionately for the day which may place them near to death again?

But the longing for health is a simple instinct, undarkened by logic.

Yet some of them have plans. Scutts has plans.

For a fortnight now he has watched for the post. "Parcel come for me, Sister? Small parcel?"

Or he will meet the postman in the corridor. "Got my eye yet?" he asks.

"What will it be like, Scutts?" we ask. "Can

you move it? Can you sleep in it? Did he match your other carefully?''

"You'll see," he says confidently. "It's grand."

"When I get my eye . . ." he says, almost with the same longing with which he says, "When I get into civies . . ."

Scutts is not one of those whose life is stopped; he has made plans. "When I get into civies and walk out of here . . ." His plans for six months' holiday "are all writ down in me notebook."

"But what shall you do, Scutts? Go to London?"

"London! . . . No towns fer me!"

He will not tell us what he is going to do. Secretly I believe it is something he wanted to do as a boy but thought himself a fool to carry out when he was a man: perhaps it is a sort of walking tour.

Among his eleven wounds he has two crippled arms. "I'm safe enough from death," he says (meaning France), "till it fetches me in a proper way."

Perhaps he means to live as though life were really a respite from death.

I had a day on the river yesterday.

"*I* seed yer with yer bit of erdy-furdy roun' yer neck an' yer little attachy-case," said Pinker.

"A nurse's life is one roun' of pleasure," said Pinker to the ward.

We had two operations yesterday—one on a sergeant who has won the D.C.M. and has a certificate written in gold which hangs above his bed, telling of his courage and of one particular deed; the other on a Welsh private.

I wonder what the sergeant was like before he won his D.C.M. . . .

There is something unreal about him; he is like a stage hero. He has a way of saying, "Now, my men, who is going to volunteer to fetch the dinners?" which is like an invitation to go over the top.

The men gape when he says that, then go on with their cards. It is like a joke.

Before his operation he was full of partially concealed boastings as to how he would bear it, how he would "come to" saying, "Let me get up! I can walk . . ."

I felt a sneaking wish that he should be undone and show unusual weakness.

When the moment came he did as he had said he would do—he laughed and waved good-bye as he was wheeled away; and in the afternoon when I came on duty I found him lying in his bed, conscious, looking brown and strong and un-concerned.

But he can't let well alone. . . .

As I passed up the ward to the bedside of the Welsh private I was called by the sergeant, and when I stood by his bed he whispered,

"Is that chap making a fuss over there?"

• "Evan?"

"Chap as has had an operation the same as me . . ."

"He's very bad."

"You don't find me making a fuss and my leg isn't half giving me something."

"We're not all alike, sergeant."

"Why should one make a fuss and another say nothing?"

"Is your leg hurting you a lot?"

"Yes, it is," and he screwed up his face into a grimace.

After all, he was a child. "Try to go to sleep," I said, knowing that it was his jealousy that was hurting him most.

I went to Evan.

He could do nothing with his pain, but in its tightest embraces, and crying, he lay with his large red handkerchief over his eyes.

"Oh, Evan . . . !" I said. I couldn't do anything, either.

"Oh, dear, dear, dear, dear, dear . . ." he wailed in his plaintive Welsh voice. "Oh, my dear leg, my poor leg . . ." He looked about nineteen. "Couldn't I lie on my side?"

"No, it would make it bleed."

"Would it?" He was so docile and so unhappy. The tears had run down and marked his pillow; I turned it, although the sergeant couldn't see.

"Will they give me something to make me sleep to-night?"

"Yes, Evan, at eight o'clock."

I said that because I was so sure of it, I had always seen it done. But oh, I should have made more sure . . . !

He built on it, he leant all his hopes upon it; his little clenched hands seemed to be holding my promise as firmly as though it had been my hand.

And Sister said, "No, no . . . it would be better not." "Oh, Sister, why not . . . ?" (I, the least of mortals, had made a promise belonging only to the gods. . . .)

"Oh, Sister, why not?"

Her reason was a good one: "He will want it more later in the night, and he can't have it twice."

I ran back to tell him so quickly—but one can't run back into the past.

It is wonderful to talk to men affectionately without exciting or implying love. The Utopian dreams of sixteen seem almost to be realized!

When I sew splints they come and talk to me. Scutts will sometimes talk for an hour. At first I was so proud that I dared hardly stir a finger for fear that I should frighten him away; now I am more sure of him. He never says "What?" to me, nor any longer jumps when I speak to him as though my every word must carry some command. When I sew splints and listen to Scutts or the old Scotch grocer or Monk—that squinting child of whom Pinker said, "Monk got a girl! He don' know what a girl is!"—I think, "We cannot all be efficient, but . . . this serves some end."

For they are complaining that I am not efficient. At first it hurt my pride; but it depends upon the point of view. Does one go into a ward primarily to help the patients or to help the Sister? It is not always the same thing, but one must not question discipline. . . .

To-day nine of the patients "went convalescent." They departed, hobbling and on stretchers, at two o'clock, with bursts of song, plastered hair, bright buttons, and not a regret. "You'll be able to hear a pin fall to-night, nurse," said one of them.

"I know we shall. And a tear too," I added.

But they won't listen to any such nonsense. They are going off to the little convalescent hospitals, they are going away to be treated like men; and I must laugh and shake hands and not dream of adding, "Perhaps we shall see you back again."

"No more route-marching . . . !" was the last cry I heard from the Nine.

How they hate route-marching—especially the City men, most especially Pinker! "March down the silly road," he grumbles, "sit on the silly grass and get heat-bumps."

Sometimes I think that sewing splints will be my undoing. If I listen much longer I shall see crooked.

To-day they had some small bottles of stout to help us say good-bye to the Nine.

Happiness is cheap. Last night at dinner a man said as he refilled his glass with champagne, "It makes me sad to think how much happiness there is in a bottle. . . ."

The attack has begun.

"At 3.15 this morning . . . on a front of two miles. . . ."

So that is why the ward is so empty and the ambulances have been hurrying out of the yard all day. We shall get that convoy for which I longed.

When the ward is empty and there is, as now, so little work to do, how we, the women, watch each other over the heads of the men! And because we do not care to watch, nor are much satisfied with what we see, we want more work. At what a price we shall get it. . . .

Scutts and Monk talk to me while I sew, but what about the Monks, Scutts, Gayners, whose wounds will never need a dressing or a tube—who lie along a front of two miles, one on his face, another on his back?

Since 3.15 this morning a lot of men have

died. Thank God one cannot go on realizing death.

But one need not think of it. This is a ward; here are lucky ones. Even when I look at Rees, even when I look at the grocer, even when I look at the T.B. ward, I know that anything, *anything* is better than death. But I have known a man here and there who did not think so—and these men, close on death it is true, were like strangers in the ward.

For one can be close on death and remain familiar, friendly, comprehensible.

I used to think, "It is awful to die." But who knows what compliance the years will bring? What is awful is to die *young*.

A new V.A.D. came into the ward yesterday— a girl straight from home, who has never been in a hospital before.

Rees told me, "She turned her head away when she saw me arm."

"I did once, Rees."

He looked down at the almost unrecognizable twelve inches which we call "Rees's wound," and considered how this red inch had paled and the lips of that incision were drawing together. "'Tisn' no more me arm," he said at length, "than . . ." he paused for a simile. "'Tisn' me arm, it's me wound," he finally explained.

His arm is stretched out at right angles from

his bed in an iron cradle, and has been for six months.

"Last night," he said, "I felt me arm layin' down by me side, an' I felt the fingers an' tried to scratch me knee. It's a feeling that's bin comin' on for some time, but last night it seemed real."

The pain of the dressing forces Rees's reason to lay some claim to his arm, but when it ceases to hurt him he detaches himself from it to such a point that the ghost-arm familiar to all amputations has arrived, as it were, by mistake.

The new V.A.D. doesn't talk much at present, being shy, but to-night I can believe she will write in her diary as I wrote in mine: "My feet ache, ache, ache. . . ." Add to that that she is hungry because she hasn't yet learnt how to break the long stretches with hurried gnawings behind a door, that she is sick because the philosophy of Rees is not yet her philosophy, that her hands and feet grow cold and her body turns to warm milk, that she longs so to sit on a bed that she can almost visualize the depression her body would make on its counterpane, and I get a glimpse of the passage of time and of the effect of custom.

With me the sickness and the hunger and the ache are barely remembered. It makes me wonder what else is left behind. . . . The old battle is again in my mind—the struggle to feel pain, to repel the invading familiarity.

Here they come!

One convoy last night and another this morning. There is one great burly man, a sort of bear, whose dried blood has squeezed through bandages applied in seven places, and who for all that mumbles "I'm well" if one asks him how he feels.

Long before those wounds are healed he will diagnose himself better than that!

"I'm well. . . ." That's to say: "I'm alive, and I have reached this bed, and this bit of meat, and this pudding in a tin!" He answers by his standards.

But in a few days he will think, "I am alive, but I might be better . . ."; and in a few weeks, "Is this, after all, happiness?"

How they sleep, the convoy men! Watching their wounds as we dress them, almost with a grave pleasure—the passports to this wonderful sleep.

Then when the last safety-pin is in they lie back without making themselves in the least comfortable, without drawing up a sheet or turning once upon the pillow, and sleep just as the head falls.

How little women can stand! Even the convoy cannot mend the pains of the new V.A.D. I dare not speak to her: she seems, poor camel, to be waiting for the last straw.

But when we wash the bowls together we must

talk. She and I together this morning washed and scrubbed, rinsed, dried, and piled basins into little heaps, and while we washed we examined each other.

She is a born slave; in fact, I almost think she is born to be tortured. Her manner with the Sisters invites and entices them to "put upon" her. Her spiritual back is already covered with sores.

I suppose she is hungry for sympathy, but it isn't really a case in which sympathy can do as much as custom. I showed her the white butterflies, without supposing them to be very solid food.

She reminds me of the man of whom the Sister said, "He must stick it out." I might have pointed to the convoy and suggested comparisons; but one cannot rub a sore back.

Someone has applied the last straw in the night.

When I came on duty a brisk little war-hardened V.A.D. was brushing a pile of dust along the long boards to the door. The poor camel whose back is broken is as though she had never existed; either she is ill or she is banished.

Such is the secret diplomacy of these establishments that nothing is known of her except her disappearance—at least among those whom one can ask. Matron knows, Sister knows. . . . But these are the inscrutable, smiling gods.

"THE BOYS . . ."

There is only one man in the ward I don't much care for—a tall boy with a lock of fair hair and broken teeth. He was a sullen boy whose bad temper made his mouth repulsive. I say "was," for he is different now.

Now he is feeble, gentle, grateful, and he smiles as often as one looks at him.

Yesterday he went for his operation in the morning, and in the afternoon when I came on duty he was stirring and beginning to groan. Sister told me to sit beside him.

I went up to the little room of screens in which he lay, and taking a wooden chair, I slipped it in between the screen and the bed and sat down.

Is it the ether which rushes up from between his broken teeth?—is it the red glare of the turkey-twill screens?—but in ten minutes I am altered, mesmerized. Even the size of my surroundings is changed. The screens, high enough to blot out a man's head, are high enough to blot out the world. The narrow bed becomes a field of whiteness. The naked arm stretched towards me is more wonderful than any that could have belonged to a boy with dirty fair hair and broken teeth; it has sea-green veins rising along it, and the bright hairs are more silver than golden.

The life of the ward goes on, the clatter of cups for supper, the shuffling of feet clad in loose carpet-slippers, but here within he and I are living together a concentrated life.

"Oh, me back!"

"I know, I know. . . ."

Do I know? I am getting to know. For while the men are drinking their cocoa I am drinking ether. I know how the waves of the pain come up and recede; how a little sleep just brushes the spirit, but never absorbs it; how the arms will struggle up to the air, only to be covered and enmeshed again in heat and blankets.

"Was it in me lung?" (He pronounces the "g"— a Lancashire boy. . . .)

"The shrapnel?"

He nods. I hold up the piece of metal which has lain buried in him these past three weeks. It has the number 20 engraved on it. That satisfies him. The blood which has come from between his lips is in a bowl placed too high for him to see.

Through the crack in the screens the man in the bed opposite watches us unwinkingly.

Eight o'clock. . . . Here is Sister with the syringe: he will sleep now and I can go home.

If one did not forget the hospital when one leaves it, life wouldn't be very nice.

From pillar to post. . . .

The dairyman, who has been gone to another hospital these five weeks, returned to-day, saying miserably as he walked into the ward, "Me 'ead's queerer than ever." His eyes, I think, are larger too, and he has still that manner of looking as though he thought someone could do something for him.

I can't—beyond raising the smallest of tablets to him with the inscription, "Another farthing spent. . . ."

Waker had a birthday yesterday and got ten postcards and a telegram. But that is as nothing to another anniversary.

"A year to-morrow I got my wound—two o'clock to-morrow morning."

"Shall you be awake, Waker?"

"Yes."

How will he celebrate it? I would give a lot to know what will pass in his mind. For I don't yet understand this importance they attach to such an anniversary. One and all, they know the exact hour and minute on which their bit of metal turned them for home.

Sometimes a man will whisper, "Nurse . . ." as I go by the bed; and when I stop I hear, "In ten minutes it will be a twelvemonth!" and he fixes his eyes on me.

What does he want me to respond? I don't know whether I should be glad or sorry that he got it. I can't imagine what he thinks of as the minute ticks. For I can see by his words that the scene is blurred and no longer brings back any picture. "Did you crawl back or walk?"

"I . . . walked." He is hardly sure.

I know that for some of them, for Waker, that moment at two o'clock in the morning changed his whole career. From that moment his arm was paralysed, the nerves severed; from that moment football was off, and with it his particular ambition. And football, governing a kingdom, or painting a picture—a man's ambition is his ambition, and when it is wiped out his life is changed.

But he knows all that, he has had time to think of all that. What, then, does this particular minute bring him?

They think I know; for when they tell me in that earnest voice that the minute is approaching they take for granted that I too will share some sacrament with them.

Waker is not everything a man should be: he isn't clever. But he is so very brave.

After his tenth operation two days ago there was a question as to whether he should have his pluggings changed under gas or not. The discussion went on between the doctors over his bed.

But the anæsthetist couldn't be found.

He didn't take any part in the discussion such as saying, "Yes, I will stand it . . ." but waited with interest showing on his bony face, and when they glanced down at him and said, "Let's get it through now!" he rolled over to undo his safety-pin that I might take off his sling.

It was all very fine for the theatre people to

fill his shoulder chockful of pluggings while he lay unconscious on the table; they had packed it as you might stuff linen into a bag: it was another matter to get it out.

I did not dare touch his hand with that too-easy compassion which I have noticed here, or whisper to him, "It's nearly over . . ." as the forceps pulled at the stiffened gauze. It wasn't nearly over.

Six inches deep the gauze stuck, crackling under the pull of the forceps, blood and pus leaping forward from the cavities as the steady hand of the doctor pulled inch after inch of the gauze to the light. And when one hole was emptied there was another, five in all.

Sometimes, when your mind has a grip like iron, your stomach will undo you; sometimes, when you could say "To-day is Tuesday, the fifth of August," you faint. There are so many parts of the body to look after, one of the flock may slip your control while you are holding the other by the neck. But Waker had his whole being in his hands, without so much as clenching them.

When we had finished and Sister told me to wipe the sweat on his forehead, I did so reluctantly, as though one were being too exacting in drawing attention to so small a sign.

I must say that the dairyman seems to me quite mad, and I only wonder how little it is noticed.

He will sit in a chair beside Palmer for hours, raising and lowering his eyebrows and fitting imaginary gloves on to his fingers.

An inspecting general, pausing at his bed this morning, said: "A dairyman, are you? Frightened of horses, are you? Then what do you do about the cows?"

He was pleased with his own joke, and the dairyman smiled too, uncomprehendingly, his eyebrows shooting up and down like swallows' wings. Such jokes mean nothing to him; he is where no joke but his own will ever please him any more. . . .

Palmer doesn't like sitting near him, but since it is too much trouble to move he allows it—poor Palmer, who has a piece of metal somewhere in his brain and is never seen without one long hand to his aching head. He said to me yesterday when I asked him which convalescent home he was going to, "It doesn't matter. We both go to the same kind before long . . ." jerking his thumb at the dairyman. As for the latter, there surely can be no escape, but for Palmer . . .

"They won't take it out; too risky. Seen my X-ray picture?"

"No."

"You look at it. Right in the middle of the brain. Seems funny that if I say I'm willing to risk it, why they shouldn't be."

"You're willing to risk it?"

"I'm only nineteen! What's the good of my head to me! I can't remember the name of the last hospital I was at. . . ."

Ah, these hurried conversations sandwiched between my duties, when in four sentences the distilled essence of bitterness is dropped into my ear!

"Sister, what will they do with Palmer?"

"They are going to discharge him. They won't operate."

"But what will happen to him?"

"I don't know."

"But if he is willing to risk his life to save his brain, can they still refuse?"

"They won't operate."

Pinker is full of grains of knowledge. He has just discovered a wonderful justification for not getting up directly he is told off for a job.

"I never refuse a nurse," he said, as he thoughtfully picked over the potatoes ("Li'l men, li'l spuds!" he says, to excuse himself for taking all the sought-after small ones) . . . "I never refuse a nurse. But I like to finish me game of draughts first—like Drake."

Pinker notices everything. He took the grocer for a ride on the tram yesterday. " 'E got so excited he got singing 'Tipperary,' an' the blood-vessels on his neck goin' fit to burst. Weren't he, Bill?"

He appealed to Monk, whose name is George.

(By the way, I wonder when people will stop calling them "Tommy" and call them "Bill." I never heard the word "Tommy" in a soldier's mouth: he was a red-coated man. "But every mate's called 'Bill,' ain't 'e, Bill?")

From the camp across the road the words of command float in through the ward window.

"Halt!" and "Left wheel!" and "Right wheel! . . ."

They float into the ward bearing the sense of heat and dust, and of the bumping of the saddle. The dairyman has perhaps put me a bit against the camp across the road.

When the dressings are finished and we scrub the enamel bowls in the annexe, one can see all the dairymen and all the plumbers, *chefs* and shop-walkers bumping up and down in a ring amid a cloud of dust, while the voice of the sergeant cries out those things that my dairyman used to think of in his sleep.

Then the jumps go up. "Left wheel!" "Right wheel! . . ." And now, "Cross your stirrups!" One out of every four of them is clinging, grabbing, swaying.

The seventh is off! It was a long fight. . . . He went almost round the horse's neck before he fell.

We must win the war, win the war, win the war!

Every sort of price must be paid, every kind of curious coinage—the pennies and farthings of fear and despair in odd places, as well as the golden coin of life which is spent across the water.

All day long the words of command come over the ward window-sills. All day long they bump and shout and sweat and play that charade of theirs behind the guns.

All day long little men training to fill just such another hospital as ours with other little men.

But one does not say any longer, "What a strange thing is life!" for only in rare moments does the divine astonishment return.

·